Saving Money on Medicines

The Drugs Budget Handbook

Penny Blanch BPharm BSc DPhil MRPharmS
Independent Pharmaceutical Adviser

Radcliffe Medical Press

Radcliffe Medical Press Ltd
18 Marcham Road, Abingdon, Oxon OX14 1AA

British Library Cataloguing in Publication Data

A catalogue record for this book is available from the British Library.

ISBN 1 85775 433 6

Typeset by Advance Typesetting Ltd, Oxfordshire
Printed and bound by TJ International Ltd, Padstow, Cornwall

Contents

Preface

Total NHS spending on medicines in 1998–99 was over £5.5 billion, representing nearly 14% of the NHS budget. This book is written to help GPs make savings, but it will also be of use to nurses, primary care group (PCG) and primary care trust (PCT) managers, and pharmacists.

After dealing with different types of budgets and budget-setting, the book examines alternatives to prescribing, suggests non-pharmacological options and discusses the possibility of patients purchasing their own medicines. A formulary of drugs available for patients to buy over the counter (OTC) is provided, which simplifies the vast range of products on offer and enables GPs to see at a glance the type of product they can recommend with confidence, and indeed the ones they may wish to avoid! After these options have been exhausted the book outlines areas of prescribing which should be considered when choosing a particular product, and suggests some cost-effective options. The organisation of the practice is important, and one chapter is dedicated to this topic, raising questions such as whether repeat prescribing is tightly controlled, and whether a practice formulary is a good option. Finally, the sources of help available to practices are listed.

Action plan

All practices have the potential to make prescribing changes. Some will be overspent and may not have addressed the easy savings, while others may only have savings left to make in the field of preventive medicine. Whatever the stage at which a practice may be, prescribing will always be high on the agenda. Decisions need to be made about new drugs, prescribing trends need to be monitored regularly, and audits need to be conducted as new guidelines are adopted. However, for a practice which is overspent perhaps the order of events should initially be as follows.

- Ensure that there is a prescribing lead in the practice (*see* Chapter 5).

- Identify any manpower resources that are available (*see* Chapter 6).

- Determine which areas of prescribing are higher than average (*see* Chapter 6).

- Identify any easy savings (*see* Chapter 4).

- Raise awareness and obtain the commitment of all staff to address the issue.

- Implement changes (*see* Chapter 6).

The next area to address is the organisation of the practice (*see* Chapters 3 and 5).

- Check that the repeat-prescribing system is well controlled.

- Initiate thorough medication reviews if these are not up to date.

- Hold regular prescribing meetings to address formulary development/ update, clinical guidelines and audit.

- Ensure that patients are being advised appropriately about over-the-counter (OTC) drugs.

More long-term objectives include the following.

- Consider whether non-pharmacological options can be introduced (*see* Chapter 2).

- Ensure that the GP–patient relationship is such as to encourage compliance and develop concordance (*see* Chapter 5).

The last two areas are by no means the least important, and in the long term are likely to give the greatest benefits. However, they are less easy to implement, and although a start can be made on the basis of what is known now, active research in both areas should provide further pointers to the most effective ways in which these issues can be addressed in the future.

Penny Blanch
October 2000

| Getting to grips with
the drugs budget

The first step in managing a drugs budget is establishing where the money is held, whether money can be transferred from other budgets, whether savings can be kept, the penalties of overspending and the benefits of staying within budget. An understanding of how budgets are set is an advantage, as the practice can then ensure that all relevant factors, which may not be obvious to the budget-setters, are taken into account. This chapter provides an overview of all of these issues.

The unified budget: cash-limited and indicative budgets

Primary care groups (PCGs) have had unified budgets since April 1999. The unified budget includes three elements, one for commissioning health-care (i.e. the hospital and community services budget), one for General Medical Services (to cover GP costs such as staffing) and one for pre-scribing. The amount of money allocated to each element is agreed locally, and money can be transferred from prescribing to commissioning and vice versa at the PCG/primary care trust (PCT) level. The budget is 'cash-limited', so that overspends in one area must be found from savings in another, and any overall overspend is carried forward into the following year.

Prior to April 1999, non-fundholding GP practices were allocated an 'indicative budget' which was not cash-limited. The budget was not held at the health authority but was set by them. Underspending practices did not keep their savings (although they could expect to receive a local payment from the incentive scheme), and any overspend from non-fundholding practices was met by the government and practices started the new year afresh. Fundholders were allocated a cash-limited budget, any overspend in one area of the budget was found from another area, and savings could be spent by the practice.

The new unified budget means that all prescribing costs are cash-limited, and greater flexibility in using the money is now possible.

Within each PCG or PCT, individual GP practices are set their own pre-scribing budgets. These can be regarded as indicative budgets, since it is at the PCG or PCT level that the cash must be balanced. Overspending practices in one area of a PCG can be offset by underspending practices in another area.

Nurse-prescribing budgets

For PCGs, a separate indicative budget is allocated to a community trust for nurse prescribing. This is necessary because community nurses are not legally permitted to prescribe from GPs' prescribing budgets. Initially around 1% of the overall prescribing budget is set aside by the PCG for nurse pre-scribing, and this amount varies locally. However, when nurse-prescribing costs are being monitored it is the costs for each practice's patients prescribed by GPs and nurses that needs to be analysed. Concern about whether nurses are prescribing more or less than 1% is less important, as increases in nurse-prescribing costs should be mirrored by decreases in GP costs. The situation is much simpler for PCTs where community nurses and GPs are both part of the PCT and all prescribing can be from the practice-prescribing budget.

The ethical implications of a cash-limited budget

The purpose of setting prescribing budgets is to allow costs to be managed and controlled. Indicative budgets were introduced by the government some years ago in an attempt to control the ever rising drug costs. This is very much an economic tool, and it does not always sit comfortably with health professionals. NHS terms of service for GPs require them to provide drugs to meet the clinical needs of patients, and the Hippocratic ideal is one of undivided clinical loyalty to patients. There is inevitably tension because there are unlikely to be sufficient funds to provide every patient with the optimal drug for every condition. Most health authorities have policies for expensive drugs (e.g. beta interferon) and for new drugs with potentially widespread use (e.g. donepezil), and guidelines such as the Standing Medical Advisory Committee (SMAC) guidelines for lipid-lowering drugs recommend restricting treatment to high-risk patients. The cash-limited prescribing budget is therefore increasingly being managed through a 'public health perspective'. This means the development of guidelines, protocols and policies on the use of drugs with the aim of obtaining the maximum health gain for the population from a limited resource. Additions to drug budgets will increasingly be allocated to particular drugs with a known health gain, rather than to meet overall pressures on costs.

The change in emphasis from the best care for individual patients to maximal health gain for the whole population is a major cultural change and one which is not yet universally accepted. Research in the USA in 1997[1] showed that only around half of the physicians surveyed thought they should try to abide by guidelines which discouraged the use of interventions with possible but unproven benefit.

Budget-setting

Until the development of PCGs, budget-setting was done by health authority staff – frequently the pharmaceutical adviser. PCGs and PCTs now have the responsibility for setting practice-prescribing budgets, although health authority expertise can still be used. There is national guidance on budget setting, but there will be local differences in implementation. GPs have access to information on this from the PCG/PCT, and should be aware of how the budget-setting process will affect their practice and whether they are in a situation where they need to make savings over a period of time or whether they have the flexibility to make improvements in the quality of prescribing. Budgets were initially set historically. They were based on the previous year's spending, an uplift was given for inflation, and adjustments were made for changes in practice populations. More recently, budgets have been set based on the previous year's budget allocation, and this is still the norm. The reason for this was to enable practices to keep any savings they made in-year. The incentive to make savings is not very great if a practice knows the only result will be a smaller budget the following year!

Typically the allocation is the starting point for the calculations, a basic uplift is given, and adjustments are made for list-size changes and any changes in specialist drug-prescribing over the previous year. In an attempt to encourage high-spending practices to make savings and to enable low-spending practices to improve the quality of prescribing, an additional uplift is usually given to low-spending practices. Many other factors can be introduced to encourage cost-effective prescribing, such as an additional uplift for high generic prescribing.

The budget-setting process is not perfect and is unlikely ever to be so. Ideally, one should calculate the expected number of patients in each practice with particular illnesses such as asthma or schizophrenia, calculate the evidence-based prescribing cost for each illness, and thus obtain the overall budget required. In practice, such information is not available and would be inaccurate at the level of a typical practice population. Instead, formulas are developed to explain existing variations in prescribing costs. The four measures of need which were used to produce the capitation formula for the April 1999 budget allocations were identified from a multivariate regression analysis of the prescribing costs in 8500 general practices with a range of measures of deprivation, mortality, morbidity and practice characteristics.[2] The model is capable of explaining 62% of the variation in prescribing expenditure at practice level. Rice and colleagues point out that further refinements of the model are limited by current data sources, and that further advances may be achieved through the use of data at the individual patient level, should this become available in the future.[2]

The whole budget-setting process is based on prescribing units rather than list size. The prescribing unit (PU) allows for the fact that an elderly population is likely to have high prescribing costs. Patients aged 65 years or over are counted as three prescribing units, and patients under 65 years and temporary residents are counted as one. The Age Sex Temporary Resident Originated Prescribing unit (ASTROPU) is a more sophisticated measure with more age bands, and is weighted for sex. Table 1.1 shows the weightings which were updated in 1997. The total number of ASTROPUs for a practice is calculated by adding together the weighting for each patient in the list.

Table 1.1. ASTROPUs updated in 1997[3]

Age (years)	Male	Female
0–4	1.0	0.8
5–14	1.4	1.2
15–24	1.7	2.1
25–34	2.0	2.4
35–44	2.8	3.2
45–54	4.4	5.4
55–64	7.6	7.2
65–74	10.1	9.6
Over 75	11.8	10.6
Temporary residents	0.5	0.5

A further adjustment can be made for residential and nursing home patients, whereby the ASTROPUs for residential home patients are doubled and those for nursing home patients are trebled. Adjustments to the budget can then be made as a practice population changes in age structure, number of temporary residents and number of nursing home patients.

Based on the work of Rice *et al.* budget setters have recently tried to take a greater account of need, by giving practices with the greatest need a larger uplift.[2] The budget-setting guidelines from the NHS for the 1999/2000 budget included factors such as percentage of the population with permanent sickness, percentage of households with no carers, percentage of the working population who are students and percentage of 0 to 1-year-olds.

Theoretical target budgets can be calculated for each practice using indicators of need. Targets are not absolute amounts – they will vary with the size of the overall allocation, and are simply a method of dividing the available resources in such a way as to take into account the variables for need and the practice population characteristics. Nevertheless, they are very helpful. Practices with actual budgets that are higher than the target for no specific reason will be moved towards the target over a period of years, and therefore savings will be needed to prevent an overspend.

In summary, budget setting is not perfect, but expertise has built up over the years and the formulas for allocating money have become more sophisticated and take account of need. It is important to be aware of the local budget-setting process, and to know whether a practice is above or below target and how quickly the PCG/PCT aims to move budgets towards the target. Any unusual features of GP practices should be made known to the budget-setters (e.g. if the practice specialises in the care of diabetics or other high-cost groups). Practices should be aware of any special uplifts. It would be well worthwhile for a practice to put in a special effort if their generic prescribing was 59% and an extra uplift was to be given to practices achieving 60%!

Contingency funds and incentive allocations

Contingency funds are normally available to deal with overspends on the prescribing budget for reasons such as changes in list size and specialist drug spend. Prior to PCGs, such funds were held at the health authority and normally represented around 1% of the overall prescribing budget. Such funds were available to non-fundholders as well as fundholders, and could make the difference between a practice receiving or not receiving an incentive allocation. PCGs and PCTs now have their own policies on contingency funds, and practices should be aware of the circumstances in which allocations can be made.

Health authorities in the past and now PCGs/PCTs have incentive schemes to encourage cost-effective prescribing. Originally such schemes were fairly simple, and underspending practices could expect to receive an allocation to be spent within the practice on such things as medical equipment, decoration and furnishings. Incentive schemes now vary widely, but are likely to include factors relating to the quality as well as the cost of prescribing.

What the prescribing budget includes and excludes

The prescribing budget covers the cost of the total price of all drugs, appliances or reagents written on a prescription and dispensed to a patient, less a discount. The total price of the drugs is also referred to as the basic price or the net ingredient cost by the Prescription Pricing Authority (PPA).

A discount is taken from the basic drug price because when medicines are purchased from wholesalers a discount is usually given. Pharmacists therefore receive the basic price of drugs minus a discount, the size of which depends on their monthly drugs bill. The Drug Tariff is produced monthly and gives details in Part V of the discount scales. In April 2000 the discount scale ranged from 7.75% for a pharmacy with a monthly total of prices up to £125, to 13.74% for a pharmacy with a monthly total of over £150 001. For the purposes of budget-setting, the PPA calculates an average discount factor which can be applied to the whole budget.

Wholesalers do not give discounts on all drugs. Zero-discount items are listed in Part II of the Drug Tariff, and it is the pharmacist's responsibility to endorse these items to indicate that they have not received a discount.

Once the discount has been taken off the basic drug price, the cost of the drugs is then referred to as the actual price by the PPA, and monitoring information from the PPA now gives the actual drug prices.

One final complication is that an analysis is performed to check that pharmacists receive the correct reimbursement for drug costs. An example of this was seen in the financial year 1998–99, when the drug price of generic ranitidine was reduced and the Drug Tariff price reductions lagged behind, with the result that pharmacists were overpaid. This overpayment was then clawed back in the financial year 1999–2000. The actual price of drugs in 1999–2000 was therefore reduced. However, since this was the year when generic drug prices increased dramatically, the effect was not obvious!

In addition to reimbursement for the cost of drugs, pharmacists are also paid a container allowance, a professional fee and any additional fees. Table 1.2 shows an example of these amounts. These do not come out of the prescribing budget, but are taken from a national budget for pharmacy services, known as the global sum.

Table 1.2. Examples of the amounts paid to pharmacists for the dispensing service from the global sum (April 2000 Drug Tariff)

Container allowance	Drug Tariff Part IV	6.5p per prescription
Professional fee	Drug Tariff Part IIIA	97.5p per prescription
Additional fees – for example:	Drug Tariff Part IIIA	
extemporaneously dispensed liquids		1.55p
elastic hosiery, measured and fitted		1.28p

It follows that the length of the repeat-prescribing cycle does not affect the prescribing costs in general practice. For example, two 28-day prescriptions will be charged the same as one 56-day prescription.

Hospital drug budgets

The prescribing element of the unified budget includes primary but not secondary care prescribing costs. However, since the unified budget includes hospital costs, money can be vired by the PCG/PCT from primary to secondary care drug budgets and vice versa. Two factors need to be taken into account when planning any virement. First, hospitals are not charged for drugs in the same way as primary care – the Drug Tariff prices do not apply. Hospital pharmacy departments can contract with manufacturers and negotiate drug prices. These are commonly less than the manufacturer's list price or the Drug Tariff price. In the past, and to a lesser extent today, manufacturers have sold drugs very cheaply to hospitals in order to achieve a market share, as patients who are discharged on a particular drug often remain on it. Well-known examples of this were Frumil and Zantac. Because of the price differences, it may be advantageous for a PCG/PCT to shift prescribing of some items from primary to secondary care, when it is more appropriate for prescribing responsibility to be in secondary care. Examples of this could include feeds for percutaneous endoscopic gastroscopy patients and drugs for *in-vitro* fertilisation. Any change of this nature needs to be made in a planned and co-ordinated fashion, and it would be the responsibility of the PCGs/PCTs to organise it.

The second factor concerns value-added tax (VAT). Prescriptions dispensed in primary care are exempt from VAT, whereas drugs purchased in secondary care are not. Because of this, some hospitals write FP10HP prescriptions (hospital prescriptions which can be dispensed in the community) for unusually expensive drugs, as the overall drug costs are less. The implications of this for primary care are that any virement between secondary and primary care needs to take VAT into account.

Drug prices

Total NHS spending on medicines in England in 1998–99 was £5547 million, 13.8% of the total NHS expenditure. Over 5 years the average growth in the drugs bill was around 8%, although the increase in 1999 was 6.2%,[4] no doubt reflecting the considerable efforts already being made to achieve savings. The reasons for the increasing drugs bill were reported to Parliament in 1999.[5] The number of prescriptions dispensed rose mainly due to an increase in the number of items per person (the ageing population will have had an effect here). The cost per prescription also increased, primarily due to a change in product mix (i.e. to the movement of prescribing from older, cheaper drugs to newer, more expensive ones such as the newer antidepressants and the lipid-lowering drugs). The Paasche Price Index estimates the average price of drugs on the market, singling out the pure price effect. From 1992 to 1998 this index was –1.5%, indicating that pure price increases are not an important factor overall in the increasing drug costs.

The pharmaceutical company is regulated by the Pharmaceutical Price Regulation Scheme (PPRS), which is a voluntary scheme, although reserve powers were included in the Health Act 1999 for those companies that may decide not to sign up or to comply. It covers licensed branded preparations, which account for around 80% by value of pharmaceutical sales to the NHS. Companies are free to determine the prices that they charge for new medicines, but the scheme regulates the level of profit made. Price increases should be approved by government. The objective of the scheme is to secure the provision of safe and effective medicines for the NHS at reasonable prices, and at the same time to promote a strong and profitable pharmaceutical industry. As well as the PPRS scheme, normal market forces of competition apply. The overall result tends to be that drug prices remain fairly stable, and the year-on-year inflationary price rises seen with other items tend not to occur.

Competition can be very effective in limiting drug costs. In recent years new drugs similar to existing products ('me-too' drugs) have been priced lower than the leading product (e.g. Zoton was launched at a lower price than Losec). Branded products have also undergone price reductions as a result of competition (e.g. Losec and Lustral). The main price reductions of course occur following patent expiry when generic products become available. Patent expiries which have had a significant effect on the drug budget have included Zantac and Capoten. Figures 1.1 and 1.2 show how the Drug Tariff prices changed over time. The price of ranitidine came down fairly slowly, and there was a period during which the Drug Tariff price could not be agreed. In contrast, the price of captopril dropped very significantly and quickly. Ranitidine now costs 37% less than its pre-patent price after three years, and captopril cost 68% less than its pre-patent price after one year.

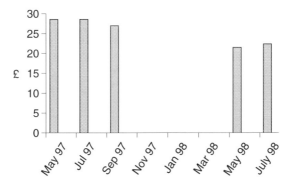

Figure 1.1   Changes in Drug Tariff price for 60 ranitidine 150 mg.

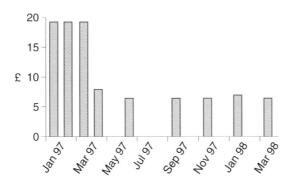

Figure 1.2   Changes in Drug Tariff price for 100 captopril 12.5 mg.

Generic prices are limited by competition, and large price increases are unusual. Indeed, some prices have remained remarkably static. The Drug Tariff price of methylpenicillin V tablets in 1963 was the equivalent of 1.2p per tablet, and in 1993 it was 1.65p per tablet – an insignificant increase over 30 years compared to the rate of inflation. The year 1999 saw a huge increase in prices following a supply problem which was estimated to have cost the NHS around £200 million.[6] The introduction of patient packs over this time will also have contributed to some price increases. Government action on the price rises is planned to reduce prices back to the average over the period November 1998 to January 1999.[6]

In summary, the implication is that GPs have the potential to make savings on the primary care drugs budget. The number of prescriptions written and the choice of drug are the most important factors in the steady increase in drug costs, and both of these are determined by the GP. Chapters 2, 3 and 5 address the potential to reduce the number of prescriptions, while Chapters 4 and 5 examine the choice of product.

References

1 Sulmasy DP *et al.* (2000) Physicians' ethical beliefs about cost-control arrangements. *Arch Intern Med.* **160**: 649–57.
2 Rice N *et al.* (2000) Derivation of a needs based capitation formula for allocating prescribing budgets to health authorities and primary care groups in England. *BMJ.* **320**: 284–8.
3 National Prescribing Centre (2000) A short guide to prescribing terms: 1999 regression analysis. *BMJ.* **320**: 284–8.
4 Jones J (2000) Lottery payout boosts NHS funds. *BMJ.* **320**: 1228.
5 Pharmaceutical Price Regulation Scheme (1999) *Third Report to Parliament. December 1999*; www.doh.gov.uk/pprs.htm
6 News (2000) Government to scrap category D and impose generic price cuts. *Pharm J.* **264**: 642.

2 Is a drug really needed?

The huge volume of drugs returned to community pharmacies for incineration suggests that some prescribing is unnecessary. One survey showed that one in ten people who collect prescriptions do not even start to take them,[1] and Wiltshire Health Authority have estimated that 2% of the drugs budget is spent on drugs which are never used.[2] Many of these drugs are returned in unbroken packages – 36% of all returned drugs were reported to be intact in one Swedish study.[3]

The following are situations in which it is not normally necessary to prescribe a drug:

- mild self-limiting conditions

- repeat prescriptions which are no longer needed

- lack of evidence of benefit of a particular drug

- the patient has no intention of taking the drug

- an alternative approach is indicated (e.g. a lifestyle change, a complementary therapy or self-medication)

- action has been taken to prevent the disease occurring.

In 1994[4] the Audit Commission reported that savings were possible because of inappropriate prescribing. Although inappropriate prescribing was not widespread, a review published in 1996[5] found sufficient inappropriate prescribing to suggest that savings could be made, even though the scope of these could not be determined. The Standing Medical Advisory Committee[6] reported that many antibiotics are prescribed unnecessarily, and a report recently produced for the NHS Executive shows that a significant proportion of prescribing for oral supplements is not for the clinical circumstances for which supplements have been recommended.[7]

However, prescribing should not be viewed in isolation. Inappropriate prescribing can and does occur, but GPs need evidence of alternatives and a knowledge of effective strategies which will reduce the need to prescribe.

This chapter explores some of the pressures on doctors that can lead to irrational prescribing and which, if recognised, could help to reduce the use of drugs. (Unnecessary prescribing caused by inadequate repeat-prescribing systems and GP–patient relationships is discussed in Chapter 5.) The chapter then discusses patient lifestyle changes and alternative medicines as potential options. Many specific examples of alternatives and successful examples of withdrawal of drug therapy are listed below in each of the main therapeutic areas.

Factors that influence prescribing

Ideally, prescribing should be for a known clinical condition and for a drug which is licensed and has a sound evidence base. The doctor should be confident in prescribing, and the patient should have sufficient knowledge to be able to take the drug correctly and to be aware of the benefits of taking the drug, and they should intend to take it. However, this is very often not the case, and the absence of any one factor could result in drug wastage. Some of these factors cannot be changed (the doctor cannot always be sure of the diagnosis), but other factors that influence prescribing are more amenable to change.

A qualitative interview study comparing high and low prescribers of benzodiazepines and minor opiates showed that high-prescribing doctors under daily pressure of prescribing volumes developed working strategies in order to cope.[8] These included allocating prescribing responsibility to other people or circumstances (e.g. the previous prescribing doctor). In reality, of course, a doctor cannot transfer prescribing responsibility. The NHS Executive has made it very clear that it is the doctor who writes the prescription who takes legal and clinical responsibility for this. Therefore the GP should question whether he or she too has developed a convenient 'working strategy' which is leading to overprescribing.

Patient demand is frequently cited as a reason for prescribing. A study in Nottingham found that patient pressure commonly influences prescribing decisions.[9] Another study in Toronto found that patient demand occurred in 48% of physician–patient encounters,[10] although almost 80% of the doctors said that patient demand did not influence their prescribing. Patient demand was found to be important when the clinical need was uncertain. A more sophisticated study showed that, rather than patient demand *per se* influencing prescribing decisions, it was the GP's perception of whether the patient wanted a prescription which was the strongest factor determining prescribing.[11] A qualitative study in Birmingham showed that prescribing decisions were informed by a concern to maintain a good relationship with the patient – doctors did not want to risk the relationship by not prescribing when a prescription was expected.[12] However, no association was found between doctors reporting this concern and their being under or over budget. The importance of the doctor–patient relationship was confirmed by a qualitative study in Manchester, where it was found to be the most important factor in deciding whether or not to prescribe.[13] The overriding concern of doctors to maintain the doctor–patient relationship and other factors concerned with the attitudes, perceptions and experience of doctors were reported as helping to explain the apparent irrationality of some prescribing decisions. The implication of this for the GP is that he or she may feel that patient demand is not influencing prescribing, but that in reality it is likely to be a significant factor and one which might, with sensitivity, be countered.

Another major influence on prescribing is the pharmaceutical company. GPs state they are not unduly influenced by pharmaceutical company representatives.[14] However, pharmaceutical companies spend enormous sums of money on large numbers of representatives, and they are unlikely to do this without a return on the investment. A meta-analysis of the effect of physician–industry interactions concluded that such interactions do affect prescribing.[15] Meetings with pharmaceutical representatives were associated with prescribing changes, and attending presentations given by pharmaceutical representative speakers was associated with non-rational prescribing. Industry communication techniques have been recognised as being successful. Indeed they are used with the objective of improving rational prescribing in Keele University's IMPACT project, which disseminates evidence-based drug information to GPs. The industry uses a variety of techniques. A study in Australia showed evidence of the following methods being used in meetings with company representatives: gifts, patient information, invitations, appeals to authority figures (e.g. claims supported by specialists) and social validation (reference to peer groups). Commitment to a product was obtained either following a direct question or through a series of questions.[16] These techniques will be very familiar to GPs in the UK. Chapter 5 addresses how this type of pressure can be managed.

Lifestyle

There is increasing awareness that lifestyle changes can be beneficial to health. The National Service Framework for Coronary Heart Disease, March 2000,[17] describes the need to increase opportunities for regular physical activity, to improve access to healthy food and to decrease unwanted exposure to other people's tobacco smoke. The introduction of specialist smoking cessation clinics is cited as an immediate priority. In the past the effect of lifestyle changes has been hampered by lack of evidence. The financial resources required to fund large clinical trials are enormous. Pharmaceutical companies invest huge sums of money on research and development, but lifestyle issues are of little interest to them. However, a considerable body of evidence has now accumulated to support a range of radical lifestyle changes.

Doctors have been prescribing exercise for some time. A study in 1996 in the USA reported that doctors were prescribing exercise in the same way that they would prescribe drugs.[18] Many health authorities have schemes for this, such as the Active Lifestyles scheme in Bromley, which is a joint scheme between the health authority and the local authority.

Exercise is known to be beneficial in a range of areas, including cardio-vascular disease, osteoporosis and depression. The exercise does not need to be vigorous, and it should be within the scope of almost everyone to participate. Patient compliance with exercise schemes can be a problem. A study in London reported that the rate of non-compliance was 78%.[19] Cost was found to be a major issue, with patients dropping out due to 'lack of money'. However, this is not as clear-cut as it appears – the low cost of the scheme did not encourage patient compliance. The real problem is that an increase in the levels of exercise will require a cultural change. Doctors can have an influence here. A questionnaire survey in the USA found that doctors could influence patients' willingness to comply by prescribing exercise and also by providing information and detailed guidance.[20] Doctors acting as role models were an important factor. Patients were much more likely to comply if the doctor exercised regularly, was of an appropriate body weight, and was a non-smoker. The author realised that this advice may not be universally welcomed!

An important practical initiative to increase the levels of exercise in a community is taking place in Sonning Common, Berkshire.[21] A GP initially tried to encourage people to walk by producing leaflets on local walks, but this was found to be ineffective. The barriers included women feeling vulnerable, stiles posing a physical barrier, and concern about getting lost. Following a community meeting, a programme of organised walks was developed. This is now a community initiative with 100 people involved every week in one of a dozen walks. Participants reported the following benefits: 10% reported a reduction in levels of illness, 25% reported a reduction in stress, 60% reported an increase in stamina and 55% reported an increase in energy levels. This initiative has been taken up by the British Heart Foundation, which aims to create 200 walking schemes over the next 5 years.

Nutrition is known to be a key factor in the development of diseases such as cardiovascular disease, cancer and osteoporosis. The general consensus on a healthy diet seems to be to eat plenty of fruit and vegetables, to avoid being too liberal with animal protein, and to avoid refined carbohydrates.[22] Resources can be a problem in getting this message across. Dietitians tend to be spread too thinly to counsel patients effectively on lipid-lowering or weight reduction strategies. In the past it was possible to prescribe drugs easily with only moderate concern about cost, yet funds were often not available for extra dietitians. This is no longer the case, since money can be moved from one budget to another with the advent of the unified budget, although a case for the cost-effectiveness of any change would have to be made.

Dietitians are useful for particular patients, but are unlikely to be the main solution to improving the overall nutrition of the population. GPs and other healthcare professionals who currently advise patients could incorporate more lifestyle advice. The public are willing to accept lifestyle advice from primary care professionals, but there is a reluctance on the part of these professionals to fulfil this role.[23] Dissatisfaction with the quality of nutrition information is perceived as a barrier to professionals providing this information. Professionals therefore need more education in this area, and they also need to be convinced of the benefits of this type of intervention, and that they can have a positive impact.

A community campaign to improve eating habits has been found to be very successful in Australia.[24] The aim was to reduce laxative use, and the campaign involved the media, social marketing principles and community activities. It resulted in a staggering 60% fall in laxative sales, and was found to be considerably more effective than a patient education campaign conducted through local doctors.

Smoking is known to be associated with a whole range of disease states, including cardiovascular disease, cancer, osteoporosis and gastrointestinal ulcers. There is evidence that brief advice from the GP does have an influence, and 'no-smoking clinics' can be very effective. However, the primary care professional's perspective in providing advice can mitigate against giving that advice. Community pharmacists participating in an audit in Bromley had the impression that their interventions were not effective until the effect was recorded in a systematic way – they remembered the strong objections to their advice, rather than the customers who accepted it (unpublished data). Prescribing for smoking prevention is not normally possible, as the majority of nicotine replacement therapies are not available on the NHS (Drug Tariff Part XV111A). There is evidence that they are effective,[25] and the price is not dissimilar to the cost of purchasing cigarettes, provided that duty is paid!

Lifestyle changes can be very beneficial. Frequently a lifestyle change that is made for one particular disease state will have a prophylactic effect on another area. For example, nutrition changes that are made in order to reduce the risk of cardiovascular disease should also reduce the likelihood of cancer, and an elderly person who takes up regular exercise to improve their mental state will find that their balance is also improved, osteoporosis will be less likely and there will be a beneficial effect on their blood pressure. It is rare that the same effect is seen with drugs, and frequently the opposite is true – one drug leading to a side-effect and another drug being prescribed. However, lifestyle changes are not the first thing one thinks of when faced with an overspent drugs budget. They will certainly help in the long term, and occasionally the effect can be rapid. However, many doctors may have implemented more obvious money-saving measures and feel that the time is now right to concentrate on lifestyle changes.

Alternative and complementary medicine

The limited funding available for assessing evidence of lifestyle changes is common to trials on alternative or complementary remedies. For example, homeopathic medicines are relatively cheap, and there is no tradition of charging higher prices to fund research. What research has been done is often criticised as being of poor quality, and the holistic approach of treating the 'whole person' is difficult to translate into the randomised clinical trial.

A second problem with alternative remedies is the cost to patients, since many of these remedies are not available on the NHS. This situation could change in the future if strong evidence of cost-effectiveness becomes available. In the meantime, some types of complementary medicine can be accessed on the NHS, but there will inevitably be local variation. Homeopathic remedies can be prescribed (although a complete homeopathy service may not be available), acupuncture is now practised in some health centres, and counselling services are often funded. Patients frequently fund alternative remedies themselves, and this can of course have a beneficial impact on the primary care drugs bill! The question that cannot be easily answered is whether a clinician can recommend alternatives with confidence.

Non-drug therapies are currently being recommended by doctors and used fairly widely by the public. A survey in Australia showed that 70% of doctors recommended non-drug therapies to patients who had been treated for anxiety or depression.[26] In the USA, a surprising 80% of family physicians refer patients to the clergy or pastoral care workers.[27] One report states that 40% of general practitioners in The Netherlands practise homeopathy, and that 42% of general practitioners in the UK refer patients to homeopaths.[28] Large numbers of the general public use alternative remedies. One report states that 30–50% of the population in industrialised nations use alternative and/or complementary medicines.[29]

Social aspects of the use of alternative remedies need to be considered. A review of the use of these therapies suggests that they empower older women. By becoming familiar with alternative therapies, older women can increase control over their own health, which leads to a greater wholeness of body, mind and spirit.[30]

Homeopathy is the subject of considerable controversy, with some clinicians refusing to believe that substances at such high dilutions can have an effect. A meta-analysis reported in 1991 concluded that the evidence is positive but that there was insufficient evidence to allow definite conclusions to be drawn.[31] Similarly, a meta-analysis of trials reported in 1997 concluded that the effect of homeopathy could not be entirely attributed to placebo, but that there was insufficient evidence for it to be concluded that homeopathy is clearly efficacious for any single clinical condition.[32] A further meta-analysis conducted in 1998 concluded that homeopathy has an effect in addition to placebo, but that this is not convincing due to methodological drawbacks and inconsistencies.[33] Such meta-analyses are themselves open to criticism. *Bandolier* pointed out that no conventional therapy would be allowed to have so many different conditions and variations grouped together in an attempt to reach a conclusion.[34] It may be that evidence for individual conditions will be forthcoming in the future, and *Bandolier* is quite positive about the effects of homeopathy in post-operative ileus.[35] However, in the meantime GPs are not in a position to recommend wholeheartedly that patients purchase homeopathic remedies with a view to reducing conventional drug use. Patients with an interest in homeopathy need not be discouraged from using these remedies, as there is some evidence of benefit, and the risk of adverse effects is extremely low.

There is evidence that certain herbal remedies are efficacious, and these will be covered in the therapeutic sections listed below. However, herbal remedies are again difficult for GPs to recommend. They act in much the same way as conventional medicines. Indeed, many conventional drugs are herbal derivatives (e.g. aspirin, morphine and digoxin). The difference is that herbal medicines usually contain a mixture of chemical substances. As one might expect, as a result of this they are not free from side-effects. This can be a real problem in general practice, especially since patients may not admit to taking alternative remedies.[36] Adverse effects are also possible due to the presence of additional ingredients such as heavy metals or corticosteroids. Conventional drugs must be licensed, and are tested for safety, efficacy and quality, whereas the regulation of herbal remedies is much less stringent. The occasions when a GP might recommend the purchase of a herbal remedy will therefore be limited to patients with a particular interest in herbal remedies, or to situations where an appropriate conventional drug is not available. As in the case of homeopathic remedies, the herbal alternative is unlikely to be significantly cost-saving.

The overall evidence for acupuncture is unclear. When trials from around the world are examined, for some countries in East Asia nearly all of the trials report positive results, whereas trials conducted in North American countries report positive results in only about half of the trials.[37]

Trials have shown acupuncture to be effective in certain conditions, and this subject will be dealt with below. Following an inquiry, the British Medical Association (BMA) has approved acupuncture, recommending that it should be made more widely available on the NHS.[38] It, too, is not free from side-effects, and there has been a report of death as a result of streptococcal toxic shock syndrome,[39] and reports of traumatic lesions with deaths occurring from pneumothorax and cardiac tamponade.[40] A recent review stated that the incidence of reported adverse events is low, with the more serious events usually being due to poor practice.[41] It concludes that acupunture is probably safe in qualified hands. The report from the BMA reaches a similar conclusion and states that complication rates are 'relatively low'.[38]

Acupuncture does have the potential to reduce the drugs budget in qualified hands, and is a potential option for conditions in which there is some evidence of benefit. If patients are seen privately, then cost is not an issue for the health service, but whether it is cost-effective to provide acupuncture on the NHS is not at all clear.

Cognitive behaviour therapy, counselling, relaxation and hypnosis also have the potential to reduce the drugs bill. Therapeutic touch seems to be a non-starter, with only one of 83 studies included in a review giving a positive effect.[42] Likewise, the use of relaxation techniques in acute and chronic pain has not been demonstrated to give pain relief,[43] and hypnotherapy has not been shown to be of positive benefit in smoking cessation.[44] A recent review of a range of mind–body practices found evidence of efficacy for musculoskeletal and related disorders, but the main conclusion was that there was a need for further research.[45] A randomised controlled trial of patients with a range of minor mental health problems showed that counselling yielded a similar benefit to conventional treatment.[46] The evidence for cognitive behaviour therapy is also positive, with a recent meta-analysis giving evidence of its efficacy in depression.[47]

In conclusion, there is some evidence for the effectiveness of particular alternative remedies. Care should be taken to recommend those with at least some documented evidence of benefit, and also to recommend suitably qualified practitioners.

Examples of alternatives to prescribing, arranged by therapeutic group

Gastrointestinal system

Withdrawal of therapy

- A systematic review published in 1994 reports that 0.5% of the population take acid-suppressing medication with a diagnosis of peptic ulcer.

It predicts significant cost savings following *Helicobacter pylori* eradication and drug discontinuation.[48] This approach has been implemented in many areas, including several King's Fund projects. Some patients can discontinue therapy, while others continue it because of reflux.

Lifestyle changes

- A qualitative study reported that patients taking proton-pump inhibitors would change their lifestyle if their GP suggested it, and that the use of these drugs led patients to abandon or not attempt lifestyle changes.[49]

- A systematic review of the use of proton-pump inhibitors and H_2-antagonists in gastro-oesophageal reflux disease reports that avoiding large meals and provocative food, drink and physical activity is probably more useful than stopping smoking, losing weight or raising the bed-head. If patients are successful in changing their lifestyle, one in five of them is likely to benefit.[50]

- Stimulant laxatives have been audited in Shropshire practices.[51] The practice with the highest prescribing rate identified poor nursing home practices of including inadequate fibre in the diet and providing little or no exercise, and was then able to exert an influence on the homes.

- A community campaign to reduce laxative use in a study in Australia resulted in a 60% reduction in laxative sales. The campaign involved the media, community activities and social marketing principles.[24]

Alternative therapies

- A randomised controlled study of a Chinese herbal remedy (with 20 components) found it to be effective in the treatment of irritable bowel syndrome.[52]

Cardiovascular system

Withdrawal of therapy

- A total of 220 residents in a nursing home in The Netherlands were identified as taking diuretics for hypertension, heart failure, ankle oedema or no reported indication. Diuretics were withdrawn in 82 cases, and the probability of patients remaining diuretic-free for at least one year was 0.47.[53]

- A review of withdrawal of antihypertensive medication reported that success rates ranged from 15% to 50%, and that factors predictive of a return to medication included high levels of pretreated blood pressure, marked obesity, short duration of treatment and left ventricular hypertrophy. Male patients were also more likely to return to medication than females.[54]

- When ambulatory blood pressure monitoring was used to withdraw antihypertensives, 6 of 25 patients who had had therapy withdrawn remained free of antihypertensive medication at 52 weeks. However, the project was not cost-effective given the cost of the particular drugs which were withdrawn.[55]

Lifestyle changes

- In total, 774 of 886 patients with a blood pressure of less than 145/85 mmHg and who were taking one antihypertensive were successfully withdrawn from therapy following interventions to reduce sodium intake and/or lose weight.[56]

- Studies have shown that exercise is beneficial. One study in Hawaii of men aged 45–68 years who were followed up for 12 years reports that walking two miles a day reduced mortality from heart disease, stroke and other causes by 50%.[57]

- A review of trials on exercise and hypertension concluded that physical activity of moderate intensity, such as walking or cycling involving rhythmic movements with the lower limbs for 50–60 min three or four times per week appeared to reduce blood pressure more effectively than vigorous exercise.[58]

- A series of organised walks initiated by a practice in Sonning Common has been successful in encouraging people to walk.[21]

- *Bandolier* reviewed a recent study on exercise and concluded that 'women who walk briskly or exercise vigorously three hours per week or more reduce the risk of heart disease'.[59]

- Motivational interviews and a financial incentive for adults aged 40–64 years resulted in increased exercise levels after 12 weeks, although this was not maintained after one year.[60]

- An educational and clinical practice audit programme for GPs on health promotion for elderly people resulted in increased levels of walking among their patients.[61]

- Alcohol appears to prevent ischaemic heart disease. The number needed to treat in order to prevent one ischaemic heart disease event has been calculated to be 24 over a period of 6 years.[62]

- A review of the evidence with regard to lipid-lowering interventions showed that the results of seven secondary prevention trials examining the effects of diet-only therapy gave a number needed to treat of 15 in order to prevent myocardial infarction or cerebrovascular death. This was similar to the results of trials of lipid-lowering drugs.[63]

- Benecol, a spread enriched with sitostanol esters, reduced total cholesterol levels by 8% – a worthwhile reduction but lower than that seen with statins.[64]

- A review of a meta-analysis showed that soya-protein intake (an average of 47 g per day) results in a reduction in serum lipids, especially in people with high initial levels.[65]

- A cohort study has shown that eating quite moderate amounts of fruit and vegetables substantially reduces the risk of stroke.[66]

- A review examining the association between homocysteine and heart disease suggested that increasing folate and vitamin B intake in the form of a multivitamin tablet may be beneficial.[22]

- Marine n-3 polyunsaturated fatty acids in fish oils retard coronary atherosclerosis, appear to prevent fatal arrhythmias and decrease mortality subsequent to myocardial infarction.[67–70]

- A doctor in the Orkneys is writing prescriptions for marinaded herrings as part of an NHS-funded project on the treatment of patients with heart disease, in order to convey the message that patients do not have to rely on drugs alone.[71]

Alternative therapies

- Two studies have suggested that *Gingko biloba* is useful in intermittent claudication.[72]

- Acupuncture is probably not beneficial in smoking cessation or the treatment of obesity.[41]

Respiratory system

Lifestyle changes

- Maternal allergen and therefore fetal allergen exposure is thought to determine whether an allergic predisposition is manifested as disease.[73] Allergen avoidance measures can be maintained in pregnancy and the first year of life.[74] Further evidence is required in this area.

- Epidemiological evidence for the role of diet, particularly intake of fruit, vegetables and fish, is increasing, but the effectiveness of dietary supplementation has not often been demonstrated.[75]

Alternative therapies

- The findings of acupuncture trials for asthma are unclear. One review states that trials have produced conflicting results,[41] while another reports that acupuncture is of significant benefit.[76]

- A randomised controlled trial of homeopathy for headache showed no difference compared to placebo.[77]

Central nervous system

Withdrawal of therapy

- Sedative/hypnotic medication was withdrawn over a two-week period in elderly women and resulted in no demonstrable effect on sleep, sleep complaints, levels of depression or daytime sleepiness.[78] A substitute pill was used to maintain the ritual of nightly pill-taking.

- Swedish nursing homes reduced the prescribing of psychotics (−19%), benzodiazepine hypnotics (−37%) and antidepressants (−59%). The intervention in the experimental group was an outreach programme designed to influence drug use through improved teamwork among physicians, pharmacists, nurses and nurses' assistants.[79]

- An audit of hypnotic use in nursing homes in Bromley showed that the most important factor determining drug use was the attitude of the person in charge, with some homes not using hypnotics at all (unpublished data).

Lifestyle changes

- A review of the value of sport in treating psychiatric illness reports that there is good evidence that exercise is effective in mild to moderate depression and in anxiety disorders.[80]

Alternative therapies

- A systematic review of eight trials assessing the efficacy of St John's wort found it to be more effective than placebo for mild to moderate depression.[81] However, the Committee on Safety of Medicines has issued a warning that St John's wort induces drug-metabolising enzymes and therefore interacts with a range of prescribed drugs.[82]

- There is good evidence for the efficacy of *Gingko biloba* in the treatment of memory impairment caused by dementia.[83,84]

- A systematic review and meta-analysis of seven trials showed that kava extract is superior to placebo in the symptomatic treatment of anxiety.[85]

- A review of the use of feverfew for migraine reports that the evidence favours its efficacy, but that its effectiveness has not been established beyond reasonable doubt.[86]

- Several randomised controlled trials support the use of acupuncture in the management of pain, especially migraine, headache and post-operative pain. There is also evidence for its usefulness in nausea and substance misuse. It is unlikely to be beneficial in smoking cessation or obesity.[41]

- A meta-analysis of cognitive therapy found that it is effective in patients with mild to moderate depression.[47] A systematic review of its use in children and adolescents also found positive effects in moderate depression.[87]

- A randomised controlled trial of counselling in primary care in patients with minor mental health problems found no difference in functional or mental health outcome between counselling and normal care by the GP.[88] A review of the evidence with regard to counselling concludes that there is insufficient evidence to recommend counselling alone in the treatment of patients with major depression.[89]

- Problem-solving treatment delivered by nurses or GPs has been shown to be effective in a randomised trial of the treatment of depression.[90]

- Randomised controlled trials of hypnosis support its use in the management of cancer pain.[91]

- The effectiveness of relaxation techniques for the treatment of acute and chronic pain is not proven.[43]

Infections

Reducing prescribing

- *Bandolier* has calculated the numbers needed not to treat for patient consultations, and reported that 'if a GP prescribed antibiotics to 100 fewer patients with throat infections in a year, 33 fewer patients would believe that antibiotics were effective, 25 fewer patients would intend to consult with the problem in the future, and 10 fewer patients would come back within the next year.'[92] Not prescribing included avoiding prescribing and delaying prescribing (by three days if treatment persisted).

- One physician has reported a reduction in antibiotic prescribing from 82.9 to 63.8 per 1000 contacts in a solo practice, and concludes that family physicians should be able to reduce their antibiotic prescribing if they are interested in doing so and have a well-established relationship with their patients.[93]

- Medical audit is reported to be a useful tool for reducing prescribing. Consultations were recorded for respiratory tract infections before and after an intervention and discussions, and the proportion of patients who were not receiving an antibiotic increased from 45% to 55%.[94]

- Following a combination of education and surveillance information from a public health virology laboratory, a study in the USA reported a 45% reduction in prescribing for upper respiratory infection and bronchitis by residents at family practice clinics.[95]

- A controlled study of GP trainees in Australia demonstrated a reduction in prescribing for upper respiratory tract infections following prescriber feedback and management guidelines.[96]

- The use of an age-appropriate sore throat score to identify Group A *Streptococcus* infection in general practice patients could result in a decrease in prescribing of antibiotics.[97]

Alternative therapies

- Cranberry juice has been studied in a randomised controlled trial involving women in whom bacteriuria with pyuria is likely to have a high incidence. *Bandolier* reported this and concluded that the addition of cranberry juice to dietary regimens in cases where urinary tract infections have a high incidence would be sensible, and that it would probably reduce the incidence of infection and the need for antibiotics.[98] However, this trial has been criticised and a review of the literature concludes that this treatment cannot be recommended.[99]

- A review on the use of yoghurt concludes that there is not enough evidence for the use of yoghurt or *Lactobacillus* to cure vaginal infections to be recommended, and at best it may have some effect in ameliorating the symptoms of bacterial vaginosis.[100]

Endocrine system

Lifestyle changes

- Physical exercise has been linked to osteoporosis. A cohort study over 21 years of men aged 44 years and over showed a reduced incidence of hip fracture in men who engaged in vigorous physical activity.[101] Exercise training programmes in women are reported to prevent or reverse bone loss by almost 1% per year compared to controls.[102] The exercise here included, for example, treadmill walking and running and some resistance and back-strengthening exercises or aerobics.

- The rate of bone loss in the elderly can be reduced and the peak bone mass in the young can possibly be increased by dietary manipulation. Changes that are likely to be of benefit include increased calcium intake, increased vitamin D intake, a moderate reduction in intake of salt, protein, caffeine and phosphate, and increased intake of potassium and magnesium.[103]

Alternative therapies

- In a review of alternative therapies for menopausal symptoms, nutritional, herbal, homeopathic and physical approaches were reviewed. There was no convincing evidence of benefit from any of these, with the exception of soy flour, for which clinical and epidemiological evidence suggests there is an effect.[104]

Malignant disease and immunosuppression

Lifestyle changes

- The findings of a large cohort study suggest a link between high folate intake and reduced colon cancer. *Bandolier* translates this into a recommendation to take a multivitamin tablet a day.[105]

- Case–control studies link the intake of whole-grain foods with cancer, the implication being that eating more than four servings of whole-grain food per week lowers the risk of many cancers by about 40%.[106]

- Frequent consumptions of salad vegetables throughout the year is considered to protect against the development of diabetes.[107]

Musculoskeletal and joint diseases

Lifestyle changes

- There is evidence that exercise benefits pain and/or functional status in patients with osteoarthritis of the hip or knee.[108]

Alternative therapies

- A review of acupuncture in rheumatological conditions concludes that there is moderately strong evidence that it may be effective in osteo-arthritis and fibromyalgia, although large-scale clinical trials have yet to be conducted.[109] However, blinded trials of acupuncture in back pain showed no difference compared to placebo,[110] and *Bandolier* reports no consistent evidence for the effectiveness of acupuncture in osteoarthritis of the knee.[108]

- There is evidence that glucosamine is effective in arthritis. A review of eight short-term trials showed no difference compared to non-steroidal anti-inflammatory drugs.[111]

- Ingestion of supplements of *n*-3 fatty acids (such as are found in fish oils) reduces both the number of tender joints and the amount of morning stiffness in patients with rheumatoid arthritis. A minimum daily dose of 3 g of eicosapentaenoic and docosahexaenoic acid is necessary.[112]

References

1 Pharmaceutical Journal (2000) Huge waste of medicines claimed. *Pharm J.* **264**: 238.
2 Pharmaceutical Journal (2000) Wiltshire Health Authority highlights medicines waste. *Pharm J.* **264**: 426.
3 Isacson D and Olofsson C (1999) Drugs up in smoke: a study of caseated drugs in Sweden. *Pharm World Sci.* **21**: 96–9.
4 Audit Commission (1994) *A Prescription for Improvement. Toward More Rational Prescribing in General Practice.* HMSO, London.
5 Buetow SA *et al.* (1996) Prevalence of potentially inappropriate long-term prescribing in general practice in the United Kingdom, 1980–95: systematic literature review. *BMJ.* **313**: 1371–4.
6 Standing Medical Advisory Committee (SMAC) (1998) *Report of the 'Path of Least Resistance' Subgroup on Antimicrobial Resistance.* Department of Health, London.
7 Norwood J *et al.* (1999) Prescribing of nutritional supplements is increasing in general practice. *BMJ.* **318**: 808.
8 Dybwad TB *et al.* (1997) Why are some doctors high prescribers of benzodiazepines and minor opiates? A qualitative study of GPs in Norway. *Fam Pract.* **14**: 361–8.
9 Macfarlane J *et al.* (1997) Influence of patients' expectations on antibiotic management of acute lower respiratory tract illness in general practice: questionnaire study. *BMJ.* **315**: 1211–14.

10 Miller E *et al.* (1999) Effects of perceived patient demand on pre-scribing anti-infective drugs. *Can Med Assoc J.* **161**: 139–42.

11 Ukoumunne O (1997) The influence of patients' hopes of receiving a prescription on doctors' perceptions and the decision to prescribe: a questionnaire survey. *BMJ.* **315**: 1506–10.

12 Stevenson FA *et al.* (1999) GPs' perceptions of patient influence on prescribing. *Fam Pract.* **16**: 255–61.

13 Bradley CP (1992) Factors which influence the decision of whether or not to prescribe: the dilemma facing general practitioners. *Br J Gen Pract.* **364**: 454–8.

14 Carthy P *et al.* (2000) A study of factors associated with cost and variation in prescribing among GPs. *Fam Pract.* **17**: 36–41.

15 Wazana A (2000) Physicians and the pharmaceutical industry: is a gift ever just a gift? *JAMA.* **283**: 373–80.

16 Roughead EE *et al.* (1998) Commercial detailing techniques used by pharmaceutical representatives to influence prescribing. *Aust N Z J Med.* **28**: 306–10.

17 National Service Framework for Coronary Heart Disease (2000) *Modern Standards and Service Models.* Department of Health, London.

18 Petrie D *et al.* (1996) Prescribing exercise for your patient. *Md Med J.* **45**: 632–7.

19 Tai SS *et al.* (1999) Promoting physical activity in general practice: should prescribed exercise be free? *J R Soc Med.* **92**: 65–7.

20 Harsha DM *et al.* (1996) Physician factors affecting patient willingness to comply with exercise recommendations. *Clin J Sport Med.* **6**: 112–18.

21 Bandolier (1999) Exercising the way to better cardiac health. *Bandolier.* **3**: 5.

22 Bandolier (1998) Homocysteine and heart disease. *Bandolier.* **57**: 3.

23 Moore H *et al.* (2000) Nutrition and the health care agenda: a primary care perspective. *Fam Pract.* **17**: 197–202.

24 Bandolier (1994) Laxatives – different aspects of the same subject. *Bandolier.* **8**: 2.

25 Bandolier (1998) Nicotine replacement. *Bandolier.* **54**: 2.

26 Harris MF *et al.* (1996) Anxiety and depression in general practice patients: prevalence and management. *Med J Aust.* **164**: 526–9.

27 Daaleman TP and Frey B (1998) Prevalence and patterns of physician referral to clergy and pastoral care providers. *Arch Fam Med.* **7**: 548–53.

28 Vallance AK (1998) Can biological activity be maintained at ultra-high dilution? An overview of homeopathy, evidence and Bayesian philosophy. *J Altern Compl Med.* **4**: 49–76.

29 Astin JA *et al.* (1998) A review of the incorporation of complementary and alternative medicine by mainstream physicians. *Arch Intern Med.* **158**: 2203–10.

30 Gaylord S (1999) Alternative therapies and the empowerment of older women. *J Women Aging.* **11**: 29–47.

31 Kleijnen J *et al.* (1991) Clinical trials of homeopathy. *BMJ.* **302**: 316–23.

32 Clausius LK *et al.* (1997) Are the clinical effects of homeopathy placebo effects? A meta-analysis of placebo-controlled trials. *Lancet.* **350**: 220.

33 Linde K and Melchart D (1998) Randomised controlled trials of individualised homeopathy: a state-of-the-art review. *J Altern Compl Med.* **4**: 371–88.

34 Bandolier (1997) Homeopathy – dilute information and little knowledge. *Bandolier.* **45**: 2.

35 Bandolier (1998) Homeopathy and postoperative ileus. *Bandolier.* **51**: 6.

36 Pettigrew AM (2000) 'Complementogenic' disease may be increasing. *BMJ.* **320**: 1341.

37 Bandolier (2000) Round the world with acupuncture. *Bandolier.* **71**: 3.

38 Silvert M (2000) Acupuncture wins BMA approval. *BMJ.* **321**: 11.

39 Ernst E and White AR (2000) Acupuncture may be associated with serious adverse effects. *BMJ.* **320**: 513.

40 Peuker ET *et al.* (1999) Traumatic complications of acupuncture. Therapists need to know human anatomy. *Arch Fam Med.* **8**: 553–8.

41 Vickers A and Zollman C (1999) Acupuncture. *BMJ.* **319**: 973–6.

42 Bandolier (1998) Bandolier's law of inverse claims. *Bandolier.* **51**: 1.

43 Bandolier (1998) Relax? Don't do it. *Bandolier.* **53**: 5.

44 Abbott NC *et al.* (2000) Hypnotherapy for smoking cessation. *Cochrane Database Syst Rev.* **2**: CD001008.

45 Luskin FM *et al.* (2000) A review of mind/body therapies in the treatment of musculoskeletal disorders with implications for the elderly. *Altern Ther Health Med.* **6**: 46–56.

46 Harvey I *et al.* (1998) A randomized controlled trial and economic evaluation of counselling in primary care. *Br J Gen Pract.* **48**: 1043–8.

47 Gloaguen V *et al.* (1998) A meta-analysis of the effects of cognitive therapy in depressed patients. *J Affect Disord.* **49**: 59–72.

48 Moore RA (1994) Helicobacter pylori *and Peptic Ulcer. A Systematic Review of Effectiveness and an Overview of the Economic Benefits of Implementing What is Known to be Effective*; http://www.jr2.ox.ac.uk/bandolier/bandopubs/hpyl/hpall.html Pain Research, Oxford.

49 Boath EH and Blenkinsopp A (1997) The rise and rise of proton-inhibitor drugs: patients' perspectives. *Soc Sci Med.* **45**: 1571–9.

50 Moore RA and Wiffen P *Systematic Review of PPI and H2A in GORD*; http://www.jr2.ox.ac.uk/bandolier/bandopubs/gordf/gord-contents.html

51 *Audit of Stimulant Laxative Prescribing in 21 Shropshire Practices* (1999); http://www.jr2.ox.ac.uk/bandolier/band65/audlax.html

52 Bandolier (1999) Herbal medicines for IBS. *Bandolier.* **60**: 7.

53 van Kraaij DJ *et al.* (1998) Use of diuretics and opportunities for withdrawal in a Dutch nursing home population. *Neth J Med.* **53**: 20–26.

54 Fletcher AE *et al.* (1988) The effect of withdrawing antihypertensive therapy: a review. *J Hypertens.* **6**: 431–6.

55 Prasad N *et al.* (1997) Safe withdrawal of monotherapy for hypertension is poorly effective and not likely to reduce health-care costs. *J Hypertens.* **15**: 1519–26.

56 Kostis JB *et al.* (1998) Does withdrawal of antihypertensive medication increase the risk of cardiovascular events? Trial of nonpharmacologic interventions in the elderly (TONE) co-operative research group. *Am J Cardiol.* **82**: 1501–8.

57 Bandolier (1998) Exercise and mortality. *Bandolier.* **50**: 2.

58 Cleroux J *et al.* (1999) Lifestlye modifications to prevent and control hypertension. 4. Recommendations of physical exercise training. *Can Med Assoc J.* **9**: S21–8.

59 Bandolier (1999) Women should walk. *Bandolier.* **68**: 3.

60 Harland J (1999) The Newcastle Exercise Project: a randomised controlled trial of methods to promote physical activity in primary care. *BMJ.* **319**: 828–32.

61 Kerse NM *et al.* (1999) Improving the health behaviours of elderly people: randomised controlled trial of a general practice education programme. *BMJ.* **319**: 683–7.

62 Bandolier (1996) Evidence-based drinking. *Bandolier.* **27**: 9.

63 Bandolier (1997) NNTs for lipid lowering. *Bandolier.* **41**: 3.

64 Bandolier (1999) Benecol and lipids. *Bandolier.* **64**: 9.

65 Bandolier (1998) Evidence-based eating. *Bandolier.* **56**: 2.

66 Bandolier (1995) Evidence-based eating. *Bandolier.* **20**: 2.

67 Angerer P and von Schacky C (2000) *n*-3 polyunsaturated fatty acids and the cardiovascular system. *Curr Opin Lipidol.* **11**: 57–63.

68 von Schacky C (2000) n-3 fatty acids and the prevention of coronary atherosclerosis. *Am J Clin Nutr.* **71**(**Supplement 1**): S224–7.

69 Marckmann P and Gronbaek M (1999) Fish consumption and coronary heart disease mortality. A systematic review of prospective cohort studies. *Eur J Clin Nutr.* **53**: 585–9.

70 Horrocks LA and Yeo YK (1999) Health benefits of docosahexaenoic acid. *Pharmacol Res.* **40**: 211–25.

71 Christie B (2000) Doctor puts herring on prescription. *BMJ.* **320**: 1361.

72 Bandolier (1995) Alternatives. *Bandolier.* **18**: 3.

73 Warner JA *et al.* (2000) Prenatal origins of allergic disease. *J Allergy Clin Immunol.* **105**: 493–8.

74 Hanrahan JP and Halonen M (1998) Antenatal interventions in childhood asthma. *Eur Respir J Suppl.* **27**: 46S–51S.

75 Smit HA *et al.* (1999) Dietary influences on chronic obstructive lung disease and asthma: a review of the epidemiological evidence. *Proc Nutr Soc.* **58**: 309–19.

76 Ziment I (2000) Recent advances in therapeutic alternatives. *Curr Opin Pulm Med.* **6**: 71–8.

77 Bandolier (1997) Another headache for homeopathy. *Bandolier.* **47**: 7.

78 Tabloski PA *et al.* (1998) A procedure for withdrawal of sleep medication in elderly women who have been long-term users. *J Gerontol Nurs.* **24**: 20–28.

79 Schmidt I *et al.* (1998) The impact of regular multidisciplinary team interventions on psychotropic prescribing in Swedish nursing homes. *J Am Geriatr Soc.* **46**: 77–82.

80 Broocks A *et al.* (1997) Value of sports in psychiatric illness. *Psychother Psychosom Med Psychol.* **47**: 379–93.

81 Gaster B and Holroyd J (2000) St John's wort for depression: a systematic review. *Arch Intern Med.* **160**: 152–6.

82 Breckenridge A (2000) *Important Interactions Between St John's Wort* (Hypericum perforatum) *Preparations and Prescribed Medicines.* Department of Health, London.

83 Wong AH *et al.* (1998) Herbal remedies in psychiatric practice. *Arch Gen Psychiatry.* **55**: 1033–44.

84 Bandolier (1998) Dementia – diagnosis and treatment. *Bandolier.* **48**: 2.

85 Pittler MH and Ernst E (2000) Efficacy of kava extract for treating anxiety: systematic review and meta-analysis. *J Clin Psychopharmacol.* **20**: 84–9.

86 Bandolier (1999) Feverfew for migraine. *Bandolier.* **65**: 9.

87 Harrington R *et al.* (1998) Systematic review of efficacy of cognitive behaviour therapies in childhood and adolescent depressive disorder. *BMJ.* **316**: 1559–63.

88 Harvey I *et al.* (1998) A randomised controlled trial and economic evaluation of counselling in primary care. *Br J Gen Pract.* **48**: 1043–8.

89 Churchill R *et al.* (1999) Should general practitioners refer patients with major depression to counsellors? Review of current published evidence. Nottingham Counselling and Antidepressants in Primary Care (CAPC) Study Group. *Br J Gen Pract.* **49**: 738–43.

90 Mynors-Wallis LM *et al.* (2000) Randomised controlled trial of problem-solving treatment, antidepressant medication, and combined treatment for major depression in primary care. *BMJ.* **320**: 26–30.

91 Sellick SM and Zaza C (1998) Critical review of five nonpharmacologic strategies for managing cancer pain. *Cancer Prev Control.* **2**: 7–14.

92 Bandolier (1997) Reducing unnecessary consultation – a case of NNNT? *Bandolier.* **44**: 4.

93 Petursson P (1996) What determines a family doctor's prescribing habits for antibiotics? A comparative study of a doctor's own behaviour in two different settings. *Scand J Prim Care.* **14**: 196–202.

94 Melander E *et al.* (1999) Medical audit changes physicians' prescribing of antibiotics for respiratory tract infections. *Scand J Prim Health Care.* **17**: 180–4.

95 Temte JL *et al.* (1999) Effects of viral respiratory disease education and surveillance on antibiotic prescribing. *Fam Med.* **31**: 101–6.

96 Zwar N *et al.* (1999) Influencing antibiotic prescribing in general practice: a trial of prescriber feedback and management guidelines. *Fam Pract.* **16**: 495–500.

97 McIsaac WJ *et al.* (1998) A clinical score to reduce unnecessary antibiotic use in patients with sore throat. *Can Med Assoc J.* **158**: 75–83.

98 Bandolier (1994) Drug watch: cranberry juice reduces bacteriuria and pyuria. *Bandolier.* **6**: 3.

99 Harkins KJ (2000) What's the use of cranberry juice? *Age and Ageing.* **29**: 9–12.

100 Bandolier (1999) Yoghurt and vaginal infections. *Bandolier.* **60**: 3.

101 Kujala UM *et al.* (2000) Physical activity and osteoporotic hip fracture risk in men. *Arch Intern Med.* **160**: 705–8.

102 Bandolier (1999) Bone mass and exercise in women. *Bandolier.* **68**: 2.

103 Swanimathan R (1999) Nutritional factors in osteoporosis. *Int J Clin Pract.* **53**: 540–48.

104 Bandolier (1998) Alternatives for the menopause. *Bandolier.* **56**: 3.

105 Bandolier (1999) Folate and colon cancer. *Bandolier.* **60**: 6.

106 Bandolier (1998) Evidence-based eating. *Bandolier.* **53**: 7.

107 Bandolier (1999) Evidence-based vegetables and diabetes. *Bandolier.* **65**: 7.

108 *Non-pharmacological interventions for osteoarthritis of the hip and knee;* http://www.jr2.ox.ac.uk/bandolier/painres/painpag/Chronrev/OARA/CP011.html

109 Berman BM *et al.* (2000) The evidence for acupuncture as a treatment for rheumatologic conditions. *Rheum Dis Clin North Am.* **26**: 103–15, ix–x.

110 Bandolier (1999) Acupuncture for back pain. *Bandolier.* **60**: 2.

111 Bandolier (1997) Glucosamine and arthritis. *Bandolier.* **46**: 2.

112 Kremer JM (2000) *n*-3 fatty acid supplements in rheumatoid arthritis. *Am J Clin Nutr.* **71**(**Supplement 1**): S349–51.

3 Can the patient buy the drug? OTC formulary

There is a significant potential to reduce the drugs budget by GPs recommending that the patient should purchase 'over-the-counter' (OTC) medicines. This chapter includes a comprehensive OTC formulary designed to make the choice of products available clearer for the GP.

Is recommending an OTC product a viable option?

OTC medicines can be recommended at the request of or with the consent of the patient. A GP's Term of Service requires medicines to be provided to meet the clinical need of patients, but this does not conflict with patients purchasing their own medicines if they wish to do so. There will of course be situations where GPs need to prescribe drugs which are available OTC, but patients who pay prescription charges are usually happy to purchase medicines directly at less cost. (A list of drugs which cost less than the prescription charge is produced by the National Pharmaceutical Association.) OTC medicines can also be purchased following an initial prescription. For instance, practices may have a policy of providing a 28-day prescription for hay fever medications. Patients will often then purchase their own medication in the following months, as it is much simpler for them to do so. Patients also frequently go to the pharmacy before consulting their GP. This is increasingly being encouraged by the government. For example, the 1999/ 2000 winter antibiotic campaign recommended people to go to the pharmacist if they had a cough, cold or sore throat,[1] and GPs can reassure patients that they are happy about this, as pharmacists will very quickly refer patients to their GP if there is cause for concern.

There is evidence that GP practices differ in the amount of OTC medicines prescribed. One study in Lincolnshire found that the prescribing of OTC medicines depended on several factors, including whether or not a practice was fundholding.[2] Fundholding practices tended to be more cost-conscious than non-fundholding practices, and this study found that GPs from fundholding practices were less likely to prescribe OTC medicines. Another study in a single fundholding practice introduced prescribing changes to reduce costs in 185 patients.[3] The changes were successful in 129 cases, of whom five patients bought their own alternative.

For the purchase of OTC medicines to be a viable option, the GP must be confident about the care that patients will receive at the pharmacy, aware of the range of medicines that can be purchased, assured that the medicines are effective, and ideally they should have reached an agreement with the local pharmacists on how referral to the pharmacy will be made. These aspects will be covered below.

Standards in the pharmacy

The pharmacists' Code of Ethics[4] requires certain standards to be met with regard to the sale of non-prescribed medicines. In particular, they have to be in a position to supervise sales of medicines, and staff selling medicines must be appropriately trained. The following is an extract from the Standards of Good Professional Practice which deals with the sale of non-prescribed medicines:[4]

Request for advice on treatment of symptoms/condition

The pharmacist or assistant must obtain sufficient information to allow an assessment to be made that the symptoms indicate that self-medication is appropriate, and to enable a suitable product or products to be recommended. Questioning using the 2-WHAM or similar approach would be suitable, and appropriate advice on the use of any recommended product must be provided (2-WHAM is W – who is it for? W – what are the symptoms? H – how long have symptoms been present? A – any action taken so far? M – any other medication?).

Request for a medicine by name

The pharmacist must ensure that the procedures for sales of medicines in the pharmacy provide for professional advice and intervention whenever this can assist in the safe and effective use of non-prescribed medicines.

The pharmacist or assistant should obtain sufficient information to allow an assessment to be made that the medicine is likely to be appropriate for the person concerned. This will normally include information about whether any other medication is being used which could interact adversely with the product requested or make that product inappropriate. The pharmacist or assistant must provide any advice which is considered appropriate to the product and the intended consumer.

Pharmacist's involvement

The procedures must ensure that the pharmacist is personally involved whenever this is necessary to provide a good standard of pharmaceutical care. Assistants should be trained to know when the pharmacist should be consulted.

Special purchasers or users

The procedures should ensure that the particular care needed is provided when supplying products for or to children, the elderly, and other special groups or individuals.

Medicines requiring special care

The pharmacist must ensure that he or she is involved in the decision to supply any medicine which requires special care to be taken. This may apply for several reasons, including the fact that the medicine has recently become available without prescription, that it may be subject to abuse or misuse, or that the licence or marketing authorisation for non-prescription use is restricted to only selected conditions.

Which medicines can be purchased OTC?

Whether or not a substance is available for sale as a medicine is determined by law, in particular by the Medicines Act 1968. The general sales list itemises medicines which can be sold in outlets other than registered pharmacies, and certain restrictions apply. For instance, the product must not have been opened since it was made up for sale so, unlike a pharmacy, a supermarket or garage cannot sell half a packet of tablets. The prescription-only sales list itemises all medicines which can only be supplied from a pharmacy in accordance with a practitioner's prescription. Medicines which are not prescription-only medicines and which do not appear on the general sales list are pharmacy medicines, and these may only be sold from a registered pharmacy under the supervision of a pharmacist. They are identified on the label by a capital 'P' in a rectangle containing no other printed matter.

Pharmacists are legally obliged to work within these restrictions, which can cause irritation and misunderstanding among the public and other professionals. Pharmacy medicines can only be sold under the supervision of a pharmacist – they must be aware of the sale and be in a position to intervene. If the pharmacist leaves the pharmacy for any reason, pharmacy sales cannot take place during that time. (Pharmacists have been known to restrict their fluid intake when the toilets are some distance from the dispensary!) Another restriction is that some medicines are pharmacy medicines for particular indications only, and with the exception of these indications they are prescription-only medicines. Hydrocortisone is a prescription-only medicine but is classified as a pharmacy medicine if it is for external use, at a maximum strength of 1%, for several specified conditions and for the use of adults or children over 10 years of age. One consequence of this can be that a medicine is available for sale in packs designed for OTC use, but larger (and potentially cheaper) dispensing packs cannot be sold.

A pharmacist is placed in a difficult situation if a doctor recommends a product outside the indications for OTC purchase. Fluconazole is a pharmacy medicine for the treatment of vaginal candidiasis in patients aged between 16 and 59 years. A pharmacist who unwittingly sells Diflucan 1 to a woman aged 65 years may find the customer returning to say that the medicine is unsuitable. The pharmacist ought not to sell the medicine in this instance, and the patient would need to go to their GP instead.

Are OTC medicines effective?

The answer is yes and no! As with all medicines, some are more effective than others and some have a much stronger evidence base than others. OTC medicines are to a large extent much the same as prescribed medicines, but of course the range of available medicines is far narrower – not that one would guess this from walking into a pharmacy, as the range of medicines on display for sale is huge. The influence of marketing pressures and legal restrictions has resulted in the limited range of available medicines being combined and packaged in such a way as to result in a confusion of products. Similar products can be marketed by the same manufacturer under different names. Examples of this include Ibutop Ralgex and Ibutop Cuprofen creams and Lemsip Cold + Flu Original Lemon and Lemsip Cold + Flu Breathe Easy. Likewise, similar products can be sold as pharmacy medicines and as general sales list medicines (e.g. Canesten cream and Canesten AF cream). Similar products are available from several different manufacturers, which is of course an advantage to the consumer as there can be significant price differentials. For example, acyclovir cream can cost between £4.15 and £5.49 (August 2000 prices), depending on the manufacturer. The OTC formulary below is an attempt to organise products in a rational way so that like products are grouped together and active ingredients can be easily identified.

The *British National Formulary (BNF)* is fairly scathing about certain medicines which are available OTC. Topical local anaesthetics and topical antihistamines are both marked as being 'less suitable for prescribing', and some OTC medicines are a combination of both. Expectorants, too, are not regarded highly. ('The assumption that sub-emetic doses of expectorants such as ammonium chloride, ipecacuanha and squill promote expectoration is a myth'.)

The dosages of some OTC preparations can result in underdosing. A person with flu who is taking Beechams All-In-One or Benylin Day and Night Cold Treatment to the recommended dose would receive only 500 mg of paracetamol four times daily.

OTC preparations can also contain unexpected drugs. A person taking Askit Powders could consume more caffeine than if they were taking Pro-Plus, and preparations such as Anadin Extra are very similar. The rationality of certain combinations could be questioned. For example, antihistamines which theoretically reduce the frequency of coughing can be found in combination with expectorants.

Despite these peculiarities with regard to some products, there are plenty of effective, single-ingredient or rational drug combination preparations from which to choose. With an awareness of the OTC products available, GPs can confidently recommend their use.

Referring to the pharmacist

GPs and other health professionals can and do refer patients to a pharmacy – often with the name of a product written on a piece of paper – without any prior discussion or agreement. However, the system will work more effectively and the GP will have more confidence in the referral if they have reached some form of agreement with the local pharmacists. It would be useful to agree whether the GP will recommend a particular product or whether they would prefer to leave the choice of product to the pharmacist. A referral note may be useful. These are available from the electronic version of *MIMS*, but could be produced in house. Boots in Leicester provided referral forms for GPs to use in conditions such as hay fever, pain relief and indigestion. A total of 101 GPs took part in the pilot project, in which they asked patients whether they would accept an OTC treatment as an alternative to a prescription.[5]

A slightly different referral trial was conducted in Bootle.[6] Here it was at the stage of patients seeking an appointment that they were asked whether they would prefer to see a pharmacist quickly rather than wait to see a doctor for any of 12 agreed conditions. However, this scheme involved the medications being prescribed free of charge for exempt patients. It is therefore likely to save the GPs time but is unlikely to make savings on the prescribing budget.

References

1 Department of Health (1999) *Antibiotics: Don't Wear Me Out.* Patient information leaflet. Department of Health, London.
2 Baines DL and Whynes DK (1997) Over-the-counter drugs and prescribing in general practice. *Br J Gen Pract.* **47**: 221–4.
3 Dowell JS *et al.* (1995) Changing to generic formulary: how one fundholding practice reduced prescribing costs. *BMJ.* **310**: 505–8.
4 Royal Pharmaceutical Society of Great Britain (1999) *Medicines, Ethics and Practice. A Guide for Pharmacists.* Royal Pharmaceutical Society of Great Britain, London.
5 Pharmaceutical Journal (1999) OTC referral scheme in Leicester. *Pharm J.* **263**: 226.
6 Pharmaceutical Journal (2000) GP–pharmacy referral trial in Bootle. *Pharm J.* **264**: 168.

An OTC formulary – the range of medicines available for sale

The OTC formulary lists drugs in a similar order to the *BNF* for easy cross-referencing. It gives information on branded and some non-branded preparations, their active constituents, indications and legal classification. Skin preparations and general antiseptic preparations are not included. Further information on the drugs, products or their legal classification can be found in the *OTC Directory* (distributed free to GPs by the Proprietary

Association of Great Britain), the *BNF* and *Medicines, Ethics and Practice. A Guide for Pharmacists* (Royal Pharmaceutical Society of Great Britain).

Legal classifications are as follows (from *Medicine, Ethics and Practice,* January 2000):

GSL – general sales list medicines

P   – pharmacy medicines (including aspirin and paracetamol pre-parations that are strictly GSL but are only available for sale in pharmacies)

PO – a medicine that contains GSL ingredients but is licensed for sale through pharmacies only.

Prices are based on the *Chemist and Druggist Monthly Price List (August 2000). Author's note*: Drug prices are subject to regular change and it is recommended that readers refer to the latest edition of the *OTC Directory* or *MIMS* for current figures.

OTC formulary

Gastrointestinal system

Antacids and other drugs for dyspepsia

Aluminium-, magnesium- and calcium-containing antacids

Aluminium hydroxide

Actal tablets GSL
Tablet containing alexitol sodium 360 mg
Relief of hyperacidity, dyspepsia and indigestion
Children: not recommended
Price: 24 £2.29, 48 £3.79, 96 £5.75

Aludrox liquid GSL
Liquid gel containing aluminium hydroxide mixture BP/Alumina 4.16% w/w
Relief of hyperacidity and indigestion
Not recommended for children under 6 years
Price: 200 ml £2.49, 500 ml £4.49

Asilone antacid tablets GSL
Tablet containing aluminium hydroxide gel dried 500 mg, simethicone 270 g
Dyspeptic symptoms of functional or organic origin, including flatulence and associated abdominal distension, heartburn including that of pregnancy, hiatus hernia and oesophagitis. Symptomatic management of gastritis and peptic ulceration
Children: not recommended
Price: 24 £2.65, 96 £7.79

Magnesium trisilicate

Magnesium trisilicate mixture BP (non-proprietary) GSL
Oral suspension containing 5% each of magnesium trisilicate, light magnesium carbonate and sodium bicarbonate; peppermint flavour

Dyspepsia

Do not give to children under 5 years

Price varies

Philips milk of magnesia GSL
Liquid containing in 5 ml magnesium hydroxide 415 mg

Relief from stomach discomfort, indigestion, overacidity, heartburn, flatulence and constipation

Children under 1 year: not recommended except on medical advice

Price: 100 ml £1.99, 200 ml £3.05

Philips milk of magnesia tablets GSL
Tablet containing magnesium hydroxide 300 mg

Relief from indigestion, nausea, biliousness, acid stomach, flatulence and heartburn

Do not give to children under 6 years

Price: 24 £1.45, 72 £2.85

Calcium carbonate

Remegel Original GSL
Tablet containing calcium carbonate 800 mg

Relief of acid indigestion, heartburn and upset stomach associated with this condition

Children: not recommended

Price: 8 £0.85, 24 £2.25, 40 £3.35 Freshmint (Alpine Mint and Lemon flavours also available)

Rennie Rap-eze GSL
Tablet containing calcium carbonate 500 mg

Symptomatic relief of indigestion, heartburn, hyperacidity, flatulence, upset stomach, dyspepsia, biliousness, over-indulgence in food and drink, indigestion during pregnancy, acid indigestion, nervous indigestion

Children: not recommended

Price: 8 £0.75, 32 £1.65, 64 £2.85

Setlers antacid peppermint tablets GSL
Tablet containing calcium carbonate 500 mg

Symptomatic relief of acid indigestion, heartburn, dyspepsia and nervous indigestion

Children: not recommended

Price: 12 £0.69, 36 £1.65, 96 £2.95

Tums Assorted Fruit Flavours GSL
Tablet containing calcium carbonate 500 mg

Symptomatic relief of acid indigestion, heartburn, flatulence, dyspepsia and nervous indigestion. Discomfort after eating

Children: not recommended

Price: 36 £1.59, 75 £2.69

Antacids containing aluminium and magnesium

Actonorm gel P
Oral suspension containing in 5 ml aluminium hydroxide 220 mg, magnesium hydroxide 200 mg and simethicone 25 mg

Treatment of dyspepsia, flatulence, indigestion and discomfort due to overeating

Price: 200 ml £4.39

Aludrox tablets GSL
Tablet containing aluminium hydroxide/magnesium carbonate co-dried 282 mg

Relief of hyperacidity and dyspepsia

Children: not recommended under 6 years

Price: 30 £2.29, 60 £3.99

Asilone antacid liquid GSL
Sugar-free suspension containing in 5 ml aluminium hydroxide 420 mg, simethicone 135 mg, magnesium oxide light 70 mg

Dyspeptic symptoms of functional or organic origin, including flatulence and associated abdominal distension, heartburn (including that of pregnancy), hiatus hernia and oesophagitis. Symptomatic management of gastritis and peptic ulceration

Children: not recommended

Price: 200 ml £3.25

Asilone suspension GSL
Sugar-free suspension containing in 5 ml aluminium hydroxide 420 mg, simethicone 135 mg, magnesium oxide light 70 mg

Dyspeptic symptoms of functional or organic origin including flatulence and associated abdominal distension, heartburn (including that of pregnancy), hiatus hernia and oesophagitis. Symptomatic management of gastritis and peptic ulceration

Children: not recommended

Price: 500 ml £4.35

Dijex suspension GSL
Suspension containing in 5 ml magnesium hydroxide 85 mg, aluminium hydroxide wet gel 4.9 g

continued overleaf

Dijex suspension GSL *(cont.)*
Symptomatic relief in acid indigestion and dyspepsia

Children: not recommended in those under 6 years

Price: 200 ml £3.19

Dijex tablets GSL
Tablet containing aluminium hydroxide/magnesium carbonate co-dried 400 mg

Relief of symptoms associated with acid indigestion and dyspepsia

Children: not recommended in those under 5 years

Price: 30 £1.85

Other compound antacid preparations

Actonorm powder P
Powder containing aluminium hydroxide gel 5%, magnesium carbonate 38.14%, calcium carbonate 14.5%, atropine sulphate 0.01%, magnesium trisilicate 5%, sodium bicarbonate 37.3%, oil of peppermint 0.05%

As an adjunct in the symptomatic relief of dyspepsia and gastro-intestinal disorders characterised by smooth muscle spasm

Children: not recommended

Price: 85 g £4.78

Andrews antacid GSL
Tablet containing calcium carbonate 600 mg, magnesium carbonate heavy 125 mg

Relief of upset stomach, heartburn, acid indigestion and trapped wind

Children: not recommended

Price: 30 £1.59, 60 £2.95 Also available in fruit flavour

Bisodol extra strong mint GSL
Tablet containing sodium bicarbonate 64 mg, calcium carbonate 522 mg, magnesium carbonate light 68 mg

Relief from indigestion, dyspepsia, heartburn, acidity and flatulence

Price: 30 £1.85

Bisodol indigestion relief powder GSL
Powder containing sodium bicarbonate 532 mg, magnesium carbonate light 345 mg, magnesium carbonate heavy 18 mg

Relief from indigestion, heartburn, dyspepsia, acidity and flatulence

Children: not recommended

Price: 100 g £3.16

Bisodol indigestion relief tablets GSL
Tablet containing calcium carbonate 522 mg, magnesium carbonate light 68 mg, sodium bicarbonate 64 mg

Relief from indigestion, heartburn, dyspepsia, acidity and flatulence

Children: not recommended

Price: 28 £1.55, 30 £1.59, 60 £2.65, 100 £3.40

continued overleaf

Bisodol wind relief GSL
Tablet containing sodium bicarbonate 63 mg, calcium carbonate 522 mg, magnesium carbonate light 68 mg, simethicone 100 mg

Relief from indigestion, dyspepsia, heartburn, acidity and flatulence

Price: 20 £2.45

Digestif Rennie peppermint flavour GSL
Tablet containing calcium carbonate 680 mg, magnesium carbonate heavy 80 mg

Relief of indigestion, heartburn, nervous indigestion, hyperacidity, flatulence, upset stomach, dyspepsia, biliousness, over-indulgence in food and drink, indigestion during pregnancy

Children: not to be given to those under 6 years

Price: 12 £0.99, 24 £1.59, 48 £2.49, 96 £3.79 Also available in spearmint and aniseed flavours

Original Andrews Salts GSL
Effervescent powder containing sodium bicarbonate 22.6% w/w, magnesium sulphate 17.4% w/w, citric acid (anhydrous) 19.5% w/w

Recommended as a laxative and as an antacid for the relief of upset stomach, indigestion and biliousness

Children: not recommended for those under 3 years

Price: 150 g £2.59, 250 g £3.59

Rennie Deflatine GSL
Tablet containing calcium carbonate 680 mg, simethicone 25 mg, magnesium carbonate heavy 80 mg

For the effective relief of acid indigestion, nervous indigestion, heartburn, upset stomach, uncomfortable bloating, biliousness, flatulence, painful trapped wind, and indigestion and heartburn during pregnancy

Price: 18 £2.99

Sodium bicarbonate-based preparations

Eno GSL
Powder containing in 5 g sodium bicarbonate 2.32 g, sodium carbonate (anhydrous) 0.5 g, citric acid 2.18 g

Symptomatic relief of indigestion, flatulence and nausea

Children: not recommended except on medical advice

Price: 150 g £3.19, 218 g £3.99, 10 sachets £1.95 Lemon Eno flavour also available

Neo gripe mixture GSL
Solution containing in 5 ml sodium bicarbonate 50 mg, dill seed oil (terpeneless) 2.5 µl, ginger tincture (strong) 10 µl

Symptomatic relief of wind pain. May also be used by nursing mothers, pregnant women and adults suffering from wind pain

Price: 150 ml £1.70

Nurse Harvey's gripe mixture GSL
Liquid containing in 5 ml sodium bicarbonate 50 mg

Symptomatic relief of wind, gripe and related pain in infants

Children: not recommended for those under 1 month old

Price: 145 ml £1.69

Woodward's gripe water GSL
Sugar- and alcohol-free liquid containing in 5 ml sodium bicarbonate 52.5 mg, dill seed oil (terpeneless) 2.3 mg

Symptomatic relief of the distress associated with wind in infants up to 1 year old

Children: not to be given to those under 1 month

Price: 150 ml £2.05

Other drugs for dyspepsia and gastro-oesophageal reflux disease

Compound alginic acid preparations

Asilone heartburn liquid GSL
Oral suspension containing in 5 ml aluminium hydroxide gel dried 80 mg, sodium alginate 220 mg, magnesium trisilicate 40 mg, sodium bicarbonate 70 mg

Relief of heartburn and acid indigestion

Children: not recommended for those under 6 years

Price: 200 ml £3.35

Asilone heartburn tablets GSL
Tablet containing aluminium hydroxide gel dried 80 mg, alginic acid 200 mg, magnesium trisilicate 40 mg, sodium bicarbonate 70 mg

Relief of heartburn and acid indigestion

Children: not recommended for those under 6 years

Price: 10 £1.10, 30 £2.55

Bisodol heartburn relief GSL
Tablet containing sodium bicarbonate 100 mg, alginic acid 200 mg, magaldrate 400 mg

Symptomatic relief of heartburn and indigestion

Children: not recommended for those under 6 years

Price: 20 £2.45

Gastrocote liquid GSL
Liquid containing in 5 ml sodium alginate 220 mg, sodium bicarbonate 70 mg, aluminium hydroxide gel dried 80 mg, magnesium trisilicate 40 mg

Relief of heartburn and acid indigestion

Children: not recommended for those under 6 years

Price: 500 ml £4.70

Gastrocote tablets GSL
Tablets containing sodium bicarbonate 79 mg, aluminium hydroxide gel dried 80 mg, magnesium trisilicate 40 mg, alginic acid 200 mg

Relief of heartburn and acid indigestion

Children: not recommended for those under 6 years

Price: 100 £6.15

continued opposite

Gaviscon 250 PO
Tablet containing sodium bicarbonate 85 mg, aluminium hydroxide 50 mg, magnesium trisilicate 12.5 mg, alginic acid 250 mg

Relief of heartburn and indigestion

Children: not to be given

Price: 24 £2.75

Gaviscon 500 PO
Tablet containing sodium bicarbonate 170 mg, aluminium hydroxide 100 mg, magnesium trisilicate 25 mg, alginic acid 500 mg

Heartburn and flatulence associated with gastric reflux, heartburn of pregnancy

Children: not to be given

Price: 12 £2.89

Gaviscon Advance PO
Oral suspension containing in 5 ml potassium bicarbonate 100 mg, sodium alginate 500 mg

Heartburn and acid indigestion

Children: not to be given except on medical advice

Price: 140 ml £3.99

Gaviscon Infant PO
Powder containing sodium alginate 225 mg, magnesium alginate 87.5 ml

Treatment for regurgitation

Children: not be given except under medical supervision

Price: 15 × 2 g £4.17

Liquid Gaviscon PO
Suspension containing in 5 ml sodium bicarbonate 133.5 mg, calcium carbonate 80 mg, sodium alginate 250 mg

Treatment of heartburn and indigestion due to gastric reflux

Children: not recommended for those aged 2–6 years except on medical advice. Not recommended for infants

Price: 100 ml £2.15, 200 ml £3.75, 500 ml £5.65 Also available in 10 ml sachets (peppermint): 12 £2.89

Rennie Duo PO
Suspension containing in 10 ml calcium carbonate 1200 mg, sodium alginate 300 mg, magnesium carbonate 140 mg

continued overleaf

Rennie Duo PO *(cont.)*
Symptomatic relief of complaints resulting from gastro-oesophageal reflux and hyperacidity, such as regurgitation and heartburn

Children: not recommended

Price: 50 ml £1.29, 180 ml £3.49, 500 ml £5.39

Setlers heartburn and indigestion liquid GSL
Suspension containing in 5 ml calcium carbonate 80 mg, sodium alginate 250 mg, sodium bicarbonate 133.5 mg

Heartburn (including that of pregnancy), dyspepsia associated with gastric reflux, hiatus hernia, reflux oesophagitis, regurgitation and all cases of epigastric and retrosternal distress where the underlying cause is gastric reflux

Children: not recommended for those under 6 years

Price: 200 ml £4.25

Activated dimeticone (simethicone) alone

Simethicone

Asilone windcheaters GSL
Soft capsule containing simethicone 100 mg
Symptomatic relief of flatulence, wind pains, bloating, abdominal distension and other symptoms associated with intestinal gas
Price: 30 £3.29

Dentinox infant colic drops GSL
Emulsified liquid with aroma of dill containing in 2.5 ml simethicone 21 mg
Wind and griping pain in infants
Price: 100 ml £2.25

Infacol GSL
Liquid containing in 1 ml simethicone 40 mg
Relief of infant colic and griping pain
Price: 50 ml £3.05

Setlers Wind-Eze gel caps GSL
Capsule containing simethicone 125 mg
Symptomatic relief of flatulence, wind pains, bloating, abdominal distension and other symptoms associated with gastrointestinal gas
Children: not recommended
Price: 20 £3.49 Chewable tablet also available: 10 £1.95, 30 £3.45

Woodward's colic drops GSL
Drops containing simethicone emulsion 23.5% w/w
Relief of symptoms of griping pain, colic or wind due to swallowed air
Price: 30 ml £2.85

Herbal preparations

Ashton and Parsons Infants' Powders GSL

White powder containing tincture of matricaria 0.002 ml

Herbal product for symptomatic relief of pain and gastric upset associated with teething

Price: 20 sachets £2.25

Indian Brandee GSL

Liquid containing cardamon tincture compound 0.187 ml, capsicum tincture (1973) 0.125 ml

Traditional herbal remedy to promote warmth and relief of flatulence and digestive discomfort

Children: not to be given

Price: 100 ml £1.69

Potter's Acidosis GSL

Tablet containing meadowsweet 160 mg, charcoal medicinal vegetable 40 mg, rhubarb 5 mg

A traditional herbal remedy for the symptomatic relief of indigestion, stomach-ache and acid stomach

Children: not recommended

Price: 60 £2.55, 100 £4.55

Antispasmodics and other drugs that alter gut motility

Antimuscarinics

Hyoscine butylbromide

Buscopan P

Tablet containing hyoscine-*N*-butylbromide 10 mg

Relief of spasm of the gastrointestinal or genito-urinary tracts and in dysmenorrhoea/period pain and for the symptomatic relief of irritable bowel syndrome

Children: not recommended for those under 6 years

Price: 20 £3.89

Other antispasmodics

Alverine

Relaxyl capsules P
Capsule containing alverine citrate 60 mg

For the relief of smooth muscle spasm of the gastrointestinal tract in irritable bowel syndrome

Children: not recommended

Price: 18 £4.95

Mebeverine

Colofac 100 P
Tablet containing mebeverine hydrochloride 100 mg

Symptomatic relief of colicky abdominal pain

Children: not recommended for those under 10 years

Price: 15 £4.99

Colofac IBS P
Tablet containing mebeverine hydrochloride 135 mg

For the symptomatic treatment of irritable bowel syndrome

Children: not recommended for those under 10 years

Price: 15 £4.99

Equilon P
Tablet containing mebeverine hydrochloride 135 mg

Symptomatic relief of irritable bowel syndrome

Children: not recommended for those under 10 years

Price: 15 £3.59

Mebeverine with ispaghula husk

Fybogel Mebeverine P
Granules containing in each sachet ispaghula husk 3.5 mg, mebeverine hydrochloride 135 mg

Treatment of abdominal pain and bowel dysfunction associated with irritable bowel syndrome or other gastrointestinal diseases

Children: not recommended

Price: 10 £4.95

Peppermint oil

Colpermin PO
Sustained release (S/R), enteric coated (E/C) capsule containing peppermint oil 0.2 ml
Symptomatic relief of irritable bowel syndrome
Children: not suitable for those under 15 years
Price: 20 £4.85, 100 £19.32

Equilon herbal GSL
E/C capsule containing peppermint oil BP 0.2 ml
Symptomatic relief of irritable bowel syndrome
Children: not recommended
Price: 12 £3.59

Mintec capsules GSL
E/C capsule containing peppermint oil 0.2 ml
Symptomatic relief of irritable bowel syndrome or spastic colon syndrome
Children: not recommended
Price: 12 £2.90, 25 £5.65, 84 £12.40

Motility stimulants

Domperidone

Motilium 10 P
Tablet containing domperidone maleate as domperidone base 10 mg
Relief of after-meal symptoms of fullness, epigastric bloating, belching and other stomach discomforts
Children: not recommended for those under 16 years
Price: 10 £3.95

Ulcer-healing drugs

H₂-receptor antagonists

> ### Cimetidine
>
> *Tagamet 100* P
> Tablet containing cimetidine 100 mg
> Short-term symptomatic relief of indigestion, hyperacidity and heartburn
> Prophylactic management of nocturnal and meal-induced heartburn
> Children: not to be given to those under 16 years
> Price: 12 £2.45, 24 £4.25

> ### Famotidine
>
> *Pepcid AC* P
> Tablet containing famotidine 10 mg
> Short-term symptomatic relief of heartburn, indigestion and acid indigestion
> Children: not to be given to those under 16 years
> Price: 6 £2.35, 12 £4.15

> ### Ranitidine
>
> *Zantac 75 Relief tablets* GSL
> Tablet containing ranitidine (as hydrochloride) 75 mg
> Relief of heartburn, indigestion and excess stomach acid
> Children: not to be given to those under 16 years
> Price: 6 £1.99, 12 £3.89
>
> *Zantac 75 tablets* P
> Tablet containing ranitidine (as hydrochloride) 75 mg
> Relief of heartburn, indigestion and excess stomach acid and prevention of these symptoms associated with consumption of food and drink
> Children: not to be given to those under 16 years
> Price: 24 £6.99

Antidiarrhoeal drugs

Adsorbents and bulk-forming drugs

Attapulgite

Entrotabs GSL
Tablet containing aluminium hydroxide 100 mg, attapulgite 360 mg, pectin 50 mg
Symptomatic relief of stomach upsets and diarrhoea
Children: not recommended for those under 6 years except on medical advice
Price: 24 £2.20

Antimotility drugs

Loperamide hydrochloride

Arret P
Capsule containing loperamide hydrochloride 2 mg
Symptomatic relief of acute diarrhoea
Children: not to be given
Price: 6 £2.99, 12 £5.15, 18 £6.50

Boots Diareze P
Capsule containing loperamide hydrochloride 2 mg
Symptomatic treatment of acute diarrhoea
Children: not recommended except on medical advice
Price: 6 £2.75, 12 £4.75

Diah-Limit GSL
Capsule containing loperamide hydrochloride 2 mg
Symptomatic relief of acute diarrhoea
Children: not to be given
Price: 6 £2.49

continued opposite

Diasorb P
Capsule containing loperamide hydrochloride 2 mg
Symptomatic relief of acute diarrhoea
Children: not to be given except on medical advice
Price: 10 £2.89

Diocalm Ultra P
Capsule containing loperamide hydrochloride 2 mg
Acute diarrhoea
Children: not recommended
Price: 6 £2.99, 12 £4.95

Imodium capsules P or GSL depending on pack size
Capsule containing loperamide hydrochloride 2 mg
Symptomatic relief of acute diarrhoea
Children: not to be given
Price: 6 £3.15, 8 £3.95, 12 £5.15, 18 £6.50

Imodium liquid P
Liquid containing in 5 ml loperamide hydrochloride 1 mg
Symptomatic relief of acute diarrhoea
Children: not to be given
Price: 90 ml £3.85

Imodium Plus P
Chewable tablet containing loperamide hydrochloride 2 mg, simethicone
125 mg
Diarrhoea and other symptoms of diarrhoea such as stomach cramps
and bloating
Children: not recommended
Price: 6 £3.45, 18 £7.95

Morphine containing preparations

Diocalm Dual Action P

Tablet containing morphine hydrochloride 0.395 mg, attapulgite (activated) 312.5 mg, attapulgite 187.5 mg

Occasional diarrhoea and its associated pain and discomfort

Children: not to be given to those under 6 years

Price: 20 £3.29, 40 £4.95

J Collis Browne's Mixture P

Mixture containing in 5 ml peppermint oil 1.5 µl, morphine anhydrous 1 mg

Alleviation of coughs and the symptoms of diarrhoea

Children: not to be given to those under 6 years

Price: 45 ml £3.20, 100 ml £4.40

J Collis Brown's tablets P

Tablet containing calcium carbonate 200 mg, kaolin light 750 mg, morphine hydrochloride 0.35 mg

Symptomatic relief of occasional diarrhoea

Children: not to be given to those under 6 years

Price: 18 £3.05, 36 £4.60

Other antidiarrhoeals

Bismuth subsalicylate

Pepto-Bismol P

Liquid containing bismuth subsalicylate 87.6 mg

Upset stomach, indigestion and nausea. Controls common diarrhoea

Children: not to be given to those under 6 years

Price: 120 ml £2.99, 240 ml £4.49

Laxatives

Bulk-forming laxatives

Ispaghula husk

Fybogel Lemon PO
Granules containing ispaghula husk 3.5 mg

Conditions that require a high fibre regimen. Relief of constipation and maintenance of bowel regularity

Children: not recommended for those under 6 years except on medical advice

Price: 10 £1.99 Orange flavour also available

Isogel GSL
Granules containing in 2 teaspoonsful (3.9 g) ispaghula husk 90% w/w

Treatment of constipation, diarrhoea and irritable bowel syndrome, and the management of patients with colostomies

Price: 200 g £3.99

Regulan Lemon and Lime GSL
Powder containing in each sachet ispaghula husk 3.4 g

For the relief of constipation and for patients requiring a high fibre regimen (e.g. those with irritable bowel syndrome and diverticular disease)

Children: not to be given to those under 6 years

Price: 30 £2.77 Orange flavour also available

Methylcellulose

Celevac tablets GSL
Tablet containing methylcellulose 500 mg

Simple constipation, diarrhoea, diverticular disease, ulcerative colitis, appetite control, treatment of obesity, and control of diarrhoea associated with colostomy and ileostomy

Price: 112 £4.75

Stimulant laxatives

Bisacodyl

Dulcolax suppositories P

Suppository containing bisacodyl 10 mg

Constipation, either chronic or of recent origin

Children: not recommended for those under 10 years

Price: 10 £2.60, 20 £4.65

Dulcolax suppositories for children P

Suppository containing bisacodyl 5 mg

Constipation of recent origin

Children: to be used under medical supervision only

Price: 5 £1.60

Dulcolax tablets GSL

Tablet containing bisacodyl 5 mg

Short-term relief of constipation

Children: not recommended for those under 10 years except on medical advice

Price: 10 £1.05, 20 £1.89, 60 £4.29

Senna

Califig California Syrup of Figs GSL
Liquid containing in 5 ml senna extract 2.5 mg

Relief of constipation

Children: dosages stated for 1 year and over

Price: 55 ml £2.35, 110 ml £3.85

Ex-Lax senna GSL
Chocolate bar of tablets containing in each tablet senna glycosides 60% 25 mg (equivalent to 15 mg sennosides)

Relief of constipation

Children: not recommended for those under 6 years

Price: 6 £1.02, 18 £2.20, 48 £4.59

Nylax with senna GSL
Tablets containing sennosides (total) 7.5 mg

Relieves the discomfort of constipation

Children: do not give to those under 5 years

Price: 10 £1.19, 30 £2.15

Senokot granules PO
Granules containing in one level 5 ml spoonful senna standardised 15 mg

Relief of occasional or non-persistent constipation

Children: not to be given except on medical advice

Price: 100 g £4.49

Senokot syrup PO
Syrup containing in 5 ml senna standardised 15 mg

Relief of occasional or non-persistent constipation

Children: not to be given to those under 6 years except on medical advice

Price: 100 ml £3.29

Senokot tablets PO
Tablet containing senna standardised 7.5 mg

Relief of occasional or non-persistent constipation

Children: not recommended except on medical advice

Price: 20 £1.95, 60 £4.49, 100 £5.39

Sodium picosulphate

Laxoberal P
Liquid containing in 5 ml sodium picosulphate 5 mg
Relief of constipation
Children: in those under 4 years, as recommended by the doctor
Price: 100 ml £3.25, 300 ml £7.75

Osmotic laxatives

Lactitol

Lactitol P
Powder containing lactitol monohydrate 10 g
Relief of constipation
Children: dosages stated for those over 1 year
Price: 10 £1.76

Lactulose

Duphalac solution P
Solution containing in 5 ml lactulose 3.35 mg
Treatment of constipation
Price: 200 ml £3.50

Magnesium hydroxide and liquid paraffin

Mil-Par P
Suspension containing in 5 ml magnesium hydroxide mixture 3.75 ml, liquid paraffin 1.25 ml
Temporary relief of constipation
Children: not to be given to those under 3 years
Price: 200 ml £3.15, 500 ml £5.09

Sodium sulphate

Fynnon Salt GSL
Powder containing sodium sulphate 5 g

Symptomatic relief of constipation and associated symptoms

Children: not to be given except on medical advice

Price: 200 g £2.40

Sodium potassium tartrate containing preparation

Jaap's Health Salts GSL
Powder containing per teaspoonful sodium bicarbonate 21.32% w/w, tartaric acid 20.81% w/w, sodium potassium tartrate 0.94% w/w

Symptomatic relief of indigestion and heartburn, and also acts as a mild laxative

Price: 180 g £2.99

Herbal laxatives

Califig herbal laxative tablets with senna GSL
Tablet containing senna extract 7.5 mg, dandelion 32 mg, peppermint 0.6 mg

Relief of constipation

Children: not to be given to those under 7 years

Price: 20 £1.69

Potter's cleansing herb tablets GSL
Tablet containing senna leaves tinnevelly 100 mg, aloes (cape) 45 mg, cascara bark 30 mg, dandelion root 30 mg, fennel seed 15 mg

A traditional herbal remedy for symptomatic relief of occasional constipation and feelings of bloatedness

Children: not recommended

Price: 50 £3.45

Jackson's Herbal Laxative GSL
Syrup containing in 5 ml senna concentrated infusion (BPC 1959) 0.05 ml, cascara liquid extract 0.05 ml, rhubarb concentrated infusion (BPC 1959) 0.05 ml

Symptomatic relief of occasional constipation

Children: not to be given to those under 7 years

Price: 100 ml £2.49

Local preparations for anal and rectal disorders

Soothing haemorrhoidal preparations

Anacal rectal ointment P
Ointment containing heparinoid 0.2% w/w, lauromacrogol-400 5% w/w

Symptomatic relief of haemorrhoids, perianal eczema, pruritis and anal fissure

Children: not recommended

Price: 30 g £5.36

Anacal suppositories P
Suppository containing heparinoid 4 mg, lauromacrogol-400 50 mg

Symptomatic relief of haemorrhoids, perianal eczema, pruritis and anal fissure

Children: not recommended

Price: 10 £3.67

Anodesyn ointment P
Ointment containing lidocaine hydrochloride 0.5% w/w, allantoin (BPC 1934) 0.5% w/w

Symptomatic relief of pain and irritation associated with external haemorrhoids

Children: not recommended

Price: 25 g £2.95

Anodesyn suppositories P
Suppository containing allantoin (BPC 1934) 10.25 mg, lidocaine hydro-chloride 10.25 mg

Symptomatic relief of pain and inflammation associated with haemor-rhoids

Children: not recommended

Price: 12 £2.89

Anusol cream GSL
Cream containing zinc oxide 10.75% w/w, bismuth oxide 2.14% w/w, balsam Peru 1.8% w/w

Symptomatic relief of uncomplicated internal and external haemorrhoids, pruritis ani, proctitis and fissures

Children: not recommended

Price: 23 g £3.15   *continued overleaf*

Anusol ointment GSL
Ointment containing zinc oxide 10.75% w/w, bismuth oxide 0.875% w/w, balsam Peru 1.875% w/w, bismuth subgallate 2.25% w/w

Symptomatic relief of uncomplicated internal and external haemorrhoids, pruritis ani, proctitis and fissures

Children: not recommended

Price: 25 g £3.15

Anusol suppositories GSL
Suppository containing zinc oxide 296 mg, bismuth oxide 24 mg, balsam Peru 49 mg, bismuth subgallate 59 mg

Symptomatic relief of uncomplicated internal haemorrhoids and other related ano-rectal conditions

Children: not recommended

Price: 12 £2.99, 24 £5.29

Germaloids cream GSL
Cream containing lidocaine hydrochloride 0.7% w/w, zinc oxide 6.6% w/w

Symptomatic relief of pain, swelling, irritation and itching associated with haemorrhoids and pruritis ani

Children: not recommended except on medical advice

Price: 25 g £2.95

Germaloids ointment GSL
Ointment containing lidocaine hydrochloride 0.7% w/w, zinc oxide 6.6% w/w

Symptomatic relief of pain, swelling, irritation and itching associated with haemorrhoids and pruritis ani

Children: not recommended except on medical advice

Price: 25 ml £2.95, 55 ml £4.79

Germaloids suppositories GSL
Suppository containing lidocaine hydrochloride 13.23 mg, zinc oxide 283.5 mg

Symptomatic relief of pain, swelling, irritation and itching associated with haemorrhoids and pruritis ani

Children: not recommended except on medical advice

Price: 12 £2.79, 24 £5.19

continued opposite

Preparation H ointment GSL
Ointment containing yeast cell extract 1% w/w, shark liver oil 3% w/w

Relief of symptoms of haemorrhoids such as pain, irritation and itching. Lubricant in easing painful bowel movements when the skin is dry and sore

Children: not recommended

Price: 25 g £3.05, 50 g £4.85

Preparation H suppositories GSL
Suppository containing yeast cell extract 1% w/w, shark liver oil 3% w/w

Relief of symptoms of haemorrhoids such as pain, irritation and itching. Lubricant for easing painful bowel movements

Children: not recommended

Price: 6 £1.72, 12 £2.99, 24 £5.09, 48 £8.75

Compound haemorrhoidal preparations with corticosteroids

Anusol Plus HC ointment P
Ointment containing zinc oxide 10.75% w/w, hydrocortisone acetate 0.25% w/w, bismuth oxide 0.875% w/w, balsam Peru 1.875% w/w, bismuth subgallate 2.25% w/w, benzyl benzoate 1.25% w/w

Symptomatic relief of uncomplicated internal and external haemorrhoids and pruritis ani

Children: not recommended for those under 18 years, and not to be used for longer than 7 days

Price: 15 g £3.95

Anusol Plus HC suppositories P
Suppository containing zinc oxide 296 mg, hydrocortisone acetate 10 mg, bismuth oxide 24 mg, balsam Peru 49 mg, bismuth subgallate 59 mg, benzyl benzoate 33 mg

Symptomatic relief of uncomplicated internal and external haemorrhoids and pruritis ani

Children: not recommended for those under 18 years, and not to be used for longer than 7 days

Price: 12 £4.15

Cardiovascular system

Diuretics

Ammonium chloride-containing diuretics

> #### Ammonium chloride
>
> *Aquaban* GSL
> Caffeine 100 mg, ammonium chloride 325 mg
> Mild diuretic for the relief of premenstrual water retention
> Children: not to be given
> Price: 30 £3.10

Herbal preparations

> *Potters Antitis* GSL
> Tablet containing buchu leaf 60 mg, buchu dry extract 100:39 23.4 mg, clivers dry extract 100:28 16.8 mg, couchgrass dry extract 5:1 80 mg, equisetum dry extract 5:1 12 mg, shepherd's-purse dry extract 5:1 12 mg, uva ursi dry extract 5:2 80 mg
> A herbal remedy traditionally used for symptomatic relief of urinary or bladder discomfort
> Children: not recommended
> Price: 50 £4.55, 100 £7.29

Peripheral vasodilators and related drugs

> #### Nicotinic acid derivatives
>
> *Crampex tablets* P
> Tablet containing nicotinic acid 20 mg, vitamin D_3 0.02 mg, calcium gluconate 200 mg
> For night muscle cramp
> Children: not recommended
> Price: 24 £3.65, 48 £5.49

Antiplatelet drugs

Aspirin

Aspirin (non-proprietary) GSL or P depending on pack size
Dispersible tablets containing aspirin 75 mg

An antiplatelet agent which helps to prevent blood clots in patients who have had a heart attack, stroke or heart bypass surgery, or who have angina

Children: not recommended in those under 12 years

Price varies

Lipid-regulating drugs

Ispaghula

Fybozest Orange P
Granules containing ispaghula husk 3.5 g

Reduction in mild to moderately elevated total serum cholesterol levels (6.5–7.8 mmol/l) for the maintenance of lowered levels thereafter. To be used with dietary modification

Children: not recommended

Price: 265 g £11.33

Respiratory system

Antihistamines

Non-sedating antihistamines

Acrivastine

Benadryl Allergy Relief P
Capsule containing acrivastine 8 mg

Symptomatic relief of allergic rhinitis, including hay fever, skin allergies such as hives and accompanying symptoms such as itching, swelling and redness

Not for use in those over 65 years of age

Children: not to be given

Price: 12 £4.35, 24 £7.55

Cetirizine hydrochloride

Zirtek P
Tablet containing cetirizine dihydrochloride 10 mg

Treatment of hay fever, allergic rhinitis and allergic skin conditions

Children: not recommended except on medical advice

Price: 7 £4.25

Loratadine

Clarityn Allergy P
Tablet containing loratadine 10 mg

Symptomatic relief of allergic rhinitis including hay fever, and allergic skin conditions such as urticaria (hives)

Children: not recommended

Price: 7 £4.45

Clarityn Allergy syrup P
Syrup containing in 5 ml loratadine 5 mg

Symptomatic relief of hay fever and allergic rhinitis such as sneezing, nasal discharge and itching and ocular itching and burning. Also allergic skin conditions such as urticaria (hives)

Children: dosages are stated for children over 2 years

Price: 50 ml £6.99

Sedating antihistamines

Chlorpheniramine maleate

Calimal antihistamine tablets P
Tablet containing chlorpheniramine maleate 4 mg

Symptomatic control of allergic conditions such as hay fever, vaso-motor rhinitis, urticaria, food allergies, insect bites, and pruritis ani or vulvae

Children: not recommended for those under 6 years

Price: 30 £1.99

Piriton allergy tablets P
Tablet containing chlorpheniramine maleate 4 mg

Symptomatic relief from all allergic conditions that are responsive to antihistamines including nettle rash, hives, heat rash and prickly heat, as well as reactions to food, medicines or insect bites and stings, and hay fever

Children: not recommended for those under 6 years

Price: 30 £2.85

Piriton syrup P
Syrup containing in 10 ml chlorpheniramine maleate 4 mg

Symptomatic relief from all allergic conditions that are responsive to antihistamines, including nettle rash, hives, heat rash, prickly heat, as well as reactions to food, medicines or insect bites and stings, and hay fever

Price: 150 ml £3.79

Chlorpheniramine maleate with ephedrine hydrochloride

Haymine P
S/R tablet containing ephedrine hydrochloride 15 mg, chlorpheniramine maleate 10 mg

Relief of symptoms caused by allergic conditions such as hay fever, allergic rhinitis, etc. which are responsive to antihistamines

Children: not recommended

Price: 10 £2.85, 30 £6.39

Clemastine

Aller-Eze tablets P
Tablet containing clemastine fumarate 1.34 mg
Relief from insect bites, stings, allergic skin disorders and allergic rhinitis
Children: not recommended for those under 3 years
Price: 10 £2.99, 30 £6.59

Clemastine with phenylpropanolamine

Aller-Eze Plus P
Tablet containing phenylpropanolamine hydrochloride 25 mg, clemastine fumarate 670 µg
Hay fever and other allergy symptoms associated with nasal and sinus congestion
Children: not recommended
Price: 12 £3.29, 24 £5.39

Diphenhydramine hydrochloride

Histergan syrup P
Syrup containing in 5 ml diphenhydramine hydrochloride 10 mg
Treatment of allergic conditions such as hay fever, insect bites and stings and allergic rashes
Price: 150 ml £3.97

Inhalations

Karvol decongestant capsules GSL
Capsule containing chlorbutanol 2.25 mg, pine oil sylvestris 9 mg, terpineol 66.6 mg, thymol 3.15 mg, pumilio pine oil 103.05 mg, levomenthol 35.55 mg

Symptomatic relief of nasal congestion and colds in the head

Children: not recommended for babies under 3 months

Price: 10 £2.05, 20 £3.65

Karvol decongestant drops GSL
Inhalation vapour liquid containing chlorbutanol 0.5% w/w, pine oil sylvestris 2% w/w, terpineol 14.8% w/w, thymol 0.7% w/w, pumilio pine oil 22.9% w/w, levomenthol 7.9% w/w

Symptomatic relief of nasal congestion and colds in the head

Price: 12 ml £2.69

Mackenzies Smelling Salts GSL
Volatile mixture containing ammonia liquor 880/890 8.698 g, eucalyptus oil 0.5 g

Traditionally used for the symptomatic relief of catarrh and head colds

Children: not to be used for babies under 3 months

Price: 17 ml £2.49

Mentholatum Vapour Rub GSL
Anhydrous ointment containing camphor 9% w/w, menthol 1.35% w/w, methyl salicylate 0.33% w/w

Symptomatic relief of colds, catarrh, hay fever, muscular pain and stiffness, backache, sciatica, lumbago, fibrositis, rheumatic pain, bruises, chilblains, minor skin conditions, dry and chapped skin, nettle rash, insect bites and stings, and itching

Children: not recommended for those under 1 year

Price: 30 g jar £2.15, 25 g tube £2.05

Olbas inhaler GSL
Inhalation oil containing eucalyptus oil 20% w/w, menthol 40% w/w, cajuput oil 20% w/w, peppermint oil 20% w/w

Symptomatic relief of blocked-up sinuses, catarrh, hay fever, colds and influenza

continued opposite

Children: not recommended for those under 7 years

Price: 0.7 g £2.35

Olbas oil GSL

Mixture of essential oils containing eucalyptus oil 35.45% w/w, menthol 4.1% w/w, cajuput oil 18.5% w/w, clove oil 0.1% w/w, juniper-berry oil 2.7% w/w, wintergreen oil 3.7% w/w, dementholised mint oil 35.45% w/w

Inhalation for relief of bronchial and nasal congestion caused by colds, catarrh, influenza and hay fever, rhinitis and minor infections of the respiratory tract. Local application for the symptomatic relief of muscular pain and stiffness, including backache, sciatica, lumbago, fibrositis and rheumatic pain

Children: not suitable for babies under 3 months

Price: 10 ml £2.19, 28 ml £3.99

Tixycolds cold and hayfever inhalant capsules GSL

Capsule containing turpentine oil 50 mg, camphor 60 mg, eucalyptus oil 20 mg, menthol 25 mg

Head colds, catarrh, influenza and hay fever

Children: not recommended for babies under 3 months

Price: 10 £2.09

Vicks Inhaler GSL

Nasal stick containing in each inhaler camphor 50 mg, menthol 125 mg, pine needle oil, siberian 10 mg

Relief of nasal congestion associated with allergic and infectious upper respiratory tract disorders

Price: £2.29

Vicks Vaporub GSL

Ointment containing turpentine oil 5% w/w, camphor 5% w/w, eucalyptus oil 1.5% w/w, menthol 2.75% w/w

Symptomatic relief of nasal catarrh and congestion, sore throat, and cough due to colds

Children: not to be used in babies under 6 months

Price: 50 g £2.99

continued overleaf

Woodward's Baby Chest Rub GSL
Inhalant rub containing turpentine oil 5% w/v, eucalyptus oil 2% w/v, menthol 2% w/v

For the symptomatic relief of nasal catarrh and congestion due to colds

Children: not for use in babies under 3 months

Price: 28 g £2.05

Wright's Vaporising Fluid P
Inhalant containing chlorocresol 10% w/v

Symptomatic relief of common colds, coughs and other upper respiratory tract infections

Children: not to be used in those under 2 years except on medical or pharmaceutical advice

Price: 50 ml £4.59

Cough preparations

Cough suppressants

Cough suppressant preparations

Codeine phosphate

Famel Original cough syrup P
Syrup containing in 5 ml codeine phosphate 1.9 mg, creosote 16.75 mg

Symptomatic relief of dry troublesome cough

Children: not recommended

Price: 120 ml £3.79, 200 ml £4.99

Pulmo Bailly P
Liquid containing guaiacol 75 mg, codeine 7 mg

Symptomatic relief of coughs associated with colds, bronchial catarrh, influenza and upper respiratory tract infections such as laryngitis and pharyngitis

Price: 90 ml £3.19

Dextromethorphan

Benylin Dry Cough (non-drowsy) P
Syrup containing in 5 ml dextromethorphan hydrobromide 7.5 mg

Relief of persistent, dry, irritating coughs

Children: not recommended for those under 6 years

Price: 125 ml £3.39

Cabdriver's adult cough linctus P
Syrup containing in 5 ml menthol 7 mg, dextromethorphan hydrobromide 11.5 mg, eucalyptus oil 0.0025 ml, pumilio pine oil 0.0015 ml,
terpin hydrate 11.5 mg

Relief of chesty coughs, bronchial congestion and catarrhal condition

Children: not recommended

Price: 100 ml £2.69

Covonia bronchial balsam P
Linctus containing in 5 ml menthol 2.5 mg, dextromethorphan hydrobromide 7.5 mg

Symptomatic relief in non-productive coughs such as those associated
with the common cold and bronchitis

Children: not recommended for those under 6 years

Price: 150 ml £2.59

Robitussin Dry Cough P
Liquid containing in 5 ml dextromethorphan hydrobromide 7.5 mg

Relief of persistent dry irritant cough

Children: not to be given to those under 6 years

Price: 100 ml £3.40

Robitussin Junior Persistent cough medicine P
Liquid containing in 5 ml dextromethorphan hydrobromide 3.75 mg

Relief of persistent dry irritant cough in children

Children: not recommended for those under 1 year

Price: 100 ml £2.95

Strepsils cough lozenges P
Lozenge containing dextromethorphan hydrobromide 2.5 mg

Relief of dry ticklish coughs   *continued overleaf*

Strepsils cough lozenges P *(cont.)*
Children: not recommended for those under 6 years
Price: 24 £2.55

Vicks Vaposyrup for dry coughs P
Syrup containing in 15 ml dextromethorphan hydrobromide 0.133% w/v
For calming a cough and coating and soothing the throat
Children: not to be given to those under 2 years
Price: 120 ml £2.99

Pholcodine

Pholcodine linctus (non-proprietary) P
Solution containing in 5 ml pholcodine 5 mg
A cough suppressant for the symptomatic relief of unproductive coughs
Children: not recommended for those under 5 years of age unless under medical supervision
Price varies

Benylin Children's Dry Coughs P
Sugar-free and colour-free solution containing in 5 ml pholcodine 2 mg
Symptomatic relief of dry, ticklish and unproductive coughs
Children: not recommended for those under 1 year
Price: 125 ml £3.19

Expulin dry cough linctus P
Sugar-free liquid containing in 5 ml pholcodine 10 mg
Relief of dry coughs
Children: not to be given
Price: 100 ml £2.35

Hill's Balsam dry cough liquid P
Mixture containing in 5 ml pholcodine 10 mg
Symptomatic relief of a dry, tickly or painful unproductive cough due to upper respiratory tract infection or influenza
Children: not recommended
Price: 100 ml £2.85

Pavacol D P
Sugar-free syrup containing in 5 ml pholcodine 5 mg
Symptomatic treatment of dry troublesome coughs
Children: not to be given to those under 1 year
Price: 300 ml £2.06

Tixylix Daytime P
Linctus containing in 5 ml pholcodine 4 mg
Relief of dry tickly coughs
Children: not recommended for those under 1 year
Price: 100 ml £2.89

Cough suppressant/systemic nasal decongestant preparations

Adult Meltus for dry tickly coughs and catarrh P
Sugar- and colour-free liquid containing in 5 ml dextromethorphan hydrobromide 10 mg, pseudoephedrine hydrochloride 10 mg

Symptomatic relief of dry, painful, tickly coughs and catarrh

Children: not recommended

Price: 100 ml £3.15

Bronalin dry cough elixir P
Sugar- and colour-free solution containing in 5 ml dextromethorphan hydrobromide 10 mg, alcohol 90% 1 ml, pseudoephedrine hydrochloride 10 mg

Symptomatic relief of dry tickly coughs and colds

Children: not recommended for those under 6 years

Price: 100 ml £2.49

Junior Meltus for dry tickly coughs and catarrh P
Sugar- and colour-free solution containing in 5 ml dextromethorphan hydrobromide 3.5 mg, pseudoephedrine hydrochloride 10 mg

Symptomatic relief of unproductive coughs accompanied by congestion of the upper respiratory tract

Children: not to be given to those under 2 years

Price: 100 ml £2.85

Sudafed linctus P
Liquid containing in 5 ml dextromethorphan hydrobromide 10 mg, pseudoephedrine hydrochloride 30 mg

Symptomatic relief of upper respiratory tract disorders that are responsive to a combination of a decongestant and an antitussive

Children: not recommended for those under 2 years

Price: 100 ml £3.39

Cough suppressant/antihistamine preparations

Benylin Children's Coughs and Colds P

Sugar-free and colour-free oral solution containing in 5 ml dextro-methorphan hydrobromide 5 mg, triprolidine hydrochloride 0.625 mg

Symptomatic relief of dry unproductive cough and other symptoms associated with colds in children

Children: not recommended in babies under 12 months

Price: 125 ml £3.19

Benylin Dry Coughs (original) P

Syrup containing in 5 ml dextromethorphan hydrobromide 6.5 mg, diphenhydramine hydrochloride 14 mg, levomenthol 2 mg

Relief of persistent, dry, irritating coughs

Children: not recommended for those under 6 years

Price: 125 ml £3.39

Benylin with Codeine P

Syrup containing in 5 ml codeine phosphate 5.7 mg, diphenhydramine hydrochloride 14 mg, levomenthol 1.1 mg

Relief of persistent, dry, irritating cough

Children: not recommended for those under 6 years

Price: 300 ml £8.29

Covonia Night-Time Formula P

Sugar-free liquid containing in 5 ml dextromethorphan hydrobromide 6.65 mg, diphenhydramine hydrochloride 10 mg

Night-time symptomatic relief of unproductive cough and congestive symptoms associated with colds

Children: not recommended

Price: 150 ml £2.89

Expulin Children's Cough Linctus – sugar-free P

Liquid containing in 5 ml chlorpheniramine maleate 1 mg, pholcodine 2 mg

Relief of cough in infants and children

Children: not to be given to those under 1 year

Price: 100 ml £2.35

continued overleaf

Tixylix Night-Time SF P

Linctus containing in 5 ml promethazine hydrochloride 1.5 mg, pholcodine 1.5 mg

Symptomatic relief of coughs and colds in children, especially irritating night-time cough

Children: not recommended for those under 1 year, children over 10 years or adults

Price: 100 ml £2.89

Cough suppressant/systemic nasal decongestant/antihistamine preparations

Actifed Compound Linctus P

Liquid containing in 5 ml dextromethorphan hydrobromide 10 mg, pseudoephedrine hydrochloride 30 mg, triprolidine hydrochloride 1.25 mg

Symptomatic relief of upper respiratory tract disorders that are responsive to a combination of a decongestant, an antihistamine and an antitussive

Children: not recommended for those under 2 years

Price: 100 ml £3.39

Benylin Cough and Congestion P

Syrup containing in 5 ml dextromethorphan hydrobromide 6.5 mg, pseudoephedrine hydrochloride 22.5 mg, diphenhydramine hydrochloride 14 mg, levomenthol 1.75 mg

Relief of cough and its congestive symptoms associated with colds

Children: not recommended for those under 6 years

Price: 125 ml £3.39

Dimotane Co P

Liquid containing in 5 ml codeine phosphate 10 mg, pseudoephedrine hydrochloride 30 mg, brompheniramine maleate 2 mg

Coughs associated with colds

Children: not recommended for those aged 2–4 years except on medical advice; not to be used in those under 2 years

Price: 100 ml £3.59

continued opposite

Dimotane Co Paediatric P
Liquid containing in 5 ml codeine phosphate 3 mg, pseudoephedrine hydrochloride 15 mg, brompheniramine maleate 2 mg

Coughs associated with colds and other similar conditions of the upper respiratory tract

Children: not recommended for those aged 2–4 years except on medical advice; not to be used in those under 2 years

Price: 100 ml £3.39

Expulin cough linctus – sugar-free P
Liquid containing in 5 ml chlorpheniramine maleate 2 mg, pseudoephedrine hydrochloride 15 mg, pholcodine 5 mg

Relief of cough associated with congestion of the nose and chest

Children: not to be given to those under 2 years

Price: 100 ml £2.35

Robitussin Night-Time P
Solution containing in 5 ml brompheniramine maleate 2 mg, codeine phosphate 10 mg, pseudoephedrine hydrochloride 30 mg

Cough suppressant and nasal decongestant for relief of dry coughs associated with colds and upper respiratory tract infection

Children: not recommended for those under 4 years except on medical advice

Price: 100 ml £3.55

Tixylix Cough and Cold P
Sugar- and colour-free linctus containing in 5 ml chlorpheniramine maleate 2 mg, pseudoephedrine hydrochloride 20 mg, pholcodine 5 mg

Relief of dry tickly cough, runny nose and congestion

Children: not recommended for those under 1 year

Price: 100 ml £2.89

Expectorants and/or demulcents

Expectorant and/or demulcent cough preparations

Simple linctus BP GSL
Linctus containing citric acid monohydrate 2.5% with an anise flavour; sugar-free versions are available
Relief of cough
Price varies

Simple linctus paediatric GSL
Linctus containing in 5 ml citric acid monohydrate 0.625% with an anise flavour; sugar-free versions are available
Relief of cough
Price varies

Adult Meltus expectorant for chesty coughs and catarrh GSL
Linctus containing in 5 ml guaifenesin 100 mg, cetylpyridinium chloride 2.4 mg, purified honey 500 mg, sucrose 1.75 mg
Symptomatic relief of coughs and catarrh associated with influenza, colds and mild throat infections
Children: not recommended
Price: 100 ml £3.15, 200 ml £4.65

Baby Meltus for babies' coughs GSL
Sugar- and colour-free linctus containing in 5 ml dilute acetic acid (16%) 0.42 ml
Symptomatic relief of the irritating and distressing coughs which often accompany colds
Children: dosages given from 3 months
Price: 100 ml £2.85

Beecham's Veno's cough mixture GSL
Syrup containing in 5 ml liquid glucose 3.18 g, treacle 1.35 g
Symptomatic relief of dry, irritating and unproductive cough
Children: not to be given to those under 3 years except on medical advice
Price: 100 ml £2.69

continued opposite

Beecham's Veno's expectorant GSL
Mixture containing in 5 ml guaifenesin 100 mg, liquid glucose 3 g, treacle 1.35 g

Symptomatic relief of coughs (including bronchial cough) and chesty catarrh, particularly following colds and influenza. Soothing, protective, demulcent action on a sore, irritated, tickling, inflamed throat

Children: not to be given to those under 3 years except on medical advice

Price: 100 ml £2.69, 160 ml £3.59

Beecham's Veno's Honey and Lemon GSL
Syrup containing in 5 ml liquid glucose 4 g, purified honey 0.29 g, lemon juice 0.9 ml

Symptomatic relief for tickly coughs and sore throats

Children: not to be given to those under 1 year

Price: 100 ml £2.69, 160 ml £3.59

Benylin Chesty Coughs (non-drowsy) PO
Syrup containing in 5 ml guaifenesin 100 mg, levomenthol 1.1 mg

Symptomatic relief of productive cough

Children: not recommended for those under 6 years

Price: 125 ml £3.39, 300 ml £6.79

Benylin Children's Chesty Coughs PO
Sugar-free and colour-free solution containing in 5 ml guaifenesin 50 mg

Symptomatic relief of productive coughs

Children: not recommended for those under 1 year

Price: 125 ml £3.19

Buttercup Honey and Lemon Syrup GSL
Oral liquid containing in 5 ml menthol 1.32 mg, liquid glucose 5.08 g, purified honey 0.33 mg, ipecacuanha liquid extract 13.9 mg

Relief of chesty, bronchial and dry or tickly coughs, and to soothe sore and irritated throat membranes and ease and relieve congestion

Children: not recommended for those under 1 year

Price: 75 ml £2.25, 150 ml £3.19

continued overleaf

Buttercup Infant Cough Syrup GSL
Oral liquid containing in 5 ml menthol 1.2 mg, liquid glucose 5.5 mg, ipecacuanha liquid extract 13.9 mg
Treatment of chesty, bronchial and dry or tickly coughs. Soothes sore and irritated throat membranes and eases and relieves congestion
Children: not recommended for those under 1 year
Price: 100 ml £2.49

Buttercup Syrup (original flavour) GSL
Oral liquid containing in 5 ml squill liquid extract 0.0031 ml, stronger capsicum tincture 0.0025 ml
Relief of coughs, colds, sore throats and hoarseness
Children: not recommended for those under 2 years
Price: 75 ml £2.25, 150 ml £3.19, 200 ml £4.15

Covonia Mentholated Cough Mixture GSL
Mixture containing in 5 ml menthol 4 mg, squill tincture 0.6 ml, liquorice liquid extract 0.125 ml
Symptomatic relief of productive (chesty) coughs and sore throats
Children: dosages given for children over 5 years
Price: 150 ml £2.59

Expulin Chesty Cough GSL
Sugar-free liquid containing in 5 ml guaifenesin 100 mg
Relief of productive cough
Children: not to be given to those under 3 years of age except on medical advice
Price: 100 ml £2.35

Famel Expectorant GSL
Linctus containing in 5 ml guaifenesin 50 mg
Relief of chesty coughs, catarrh and bronchial congestion
Children: not recommended for those under 1 year
Price: 120 ml £3.79, 200 ml £4.99

Fennings Little Healers GSL
Tablet containing ipecacuanha prepared 20 mg
Aid to expectoration in coughs associated with colds and catarrh
Children: not recommended for those under 5 years
Price: 36 £1.69, 90 £2.49

continued opposite

Galloway's Cough Syrup GSL
Liquid containing in 5 ml ipecacuanha liquid extract 0.0045 ml, squill vinegar 0.0267 ml

Relief of coughs and hoarseness

Price: 75 ml £2.45, 150 ml £3.35, 300 ml £4.99

Hill's Balsam Chesty Cough Liquid GSL
Mixture containing in 5 ml guaifenesin 100 mg

Relief of chesty cough in adults and children over 12 years

Children: not recommended

Price: 100 ml £2.85, 200 ml £4.29

Hill's Balsam Chesty Cough Liquid for Children GSL
Mixture containing in 5 ml citric acid (anhydrous) 20 mg, ipecacuanha liquid extract 0.01 ml

To relieve and soothe chesty coughs and bronchial catarrh in children under 12 years

Price: 100 ml £2.65

Hill's Balsam Chesty Cough Pastilles GSL
Pastille containing menthol 2.002 mg, peppermint oil 0.724 mg, ipecacuanha liquid extract 9.044 mg, benzoin tincture compound 12.719 mg

Symptomatic relief of coughs, colds and catarrh

Children: not recommended

Price: 45 g £1.91

Hill's Balsam Extra Strong '2 in 1' Pastilles GSL
Pastille containing benzoin tincture compound 3.269 mg, ipecacuanha liquid extract 8.988 mg, menthol 19.897 mg, peppermint oil 0.719 mg

Symptomatic relief of coughs, colds and catarrh

Children: not recommended

Price: 45 g £1.91

Hill's Balsam Nasal Congestion Pastilles GSL
Pastille containing eucalyptus oil 0.6% v/w, menthol 0.8% w/w

Symptomatic relief of colds and blocked nose

Price: 45 g £1.91

continued overleaf

Honey and Lemon Meltus Expectorant GSL
Syrup containing in 5 ml guaifenesin 50 mg
For symptomatic relief of deep chesty coughs and to soothe the throat
Children: not recommended for those under 2 years except on medical advice
Price: 100 ml £2.85

Jackson's All Fours GSL
Syrup containing in 5 ml guaifenesin 50 mg
For relief of chesty coughs
Children: not to be given
Price: 200 ml £1.69

Jackson's Lemon Linctus GSL
Syrup containing in 5 ml purified honey 1.5 g, glycerin 0.63 g
Symptomatic relief of sore throats and dry tickly coughs
Price: 100 ml £1.69

Junior Meltus expectorant for chesty coughs and catarrh GSL
Liquid containing in 5 ml guaifenesin 50 mg, purified honey 500 mg, cetylpyridinium chloride 2.5 mg, sucrose 2 g
Symptomatic relief of coughs and catarrh associated with influenza, colds and mild throat infections
Children: not recommended for those under 1 year except on medical advice
Price: 100 ml £2.85

Junior Meltus sugar- and colour-free expectorant GSL
Liquid containing in 5 ml guaifenesin 50 mg, cetylpyridinium chloride 2.5 ml
Symptomatic relief of coughs and catarrh associated with influenza, colds and mild throat infections
Children: not recommended for those under 1 year except on medical advice
Price: 100 ml £2.85

Lemsip Cough + Cold Chesty Cough GSL
Linctus containing in 5 ml guaifenesin 50 mg
For symptomatic relief of deep chesty coughs and to soothe the throat
Children: not to be given to those under 2 years
Price: 100 ml £2.49   *continued opposite*

Lemsip Cough + Cold Dry Cough GSL
Linctus containing in 5 ml purified honey 500 mg, glycerin 0.25 ml, citric acid 25 mg, lemon oil terpeneless 50 μl, syrup 3.75 ml

Symptomatic relief of dry tickly cough and sore throats

Price: 100 ml £2.49

Liquifruta Garlic Cough Medicine GSL
Liquid containing in 10 ml guaifenesin 100 mg

Relief of chesty coughs, hoarseness and sore throats associated with upper respiratory tract infections

Price: 75 ml £2.59, 150 ml £3.65

Meggazones GSL
Pastilles containing menthol 16 mg

Symptomatic relief of sore throats, coughs, colds, catarrh and nasal congestion

Price: 24 £2.15

Nurse Sykes bronchial balsam GSL
Liquid containing in 5 ml guaifenesin 100 mg

Symptomatic relief of bronchial catarrh and ticklish (night-time) coughs

Children: not to be given

Price: 100 ml £1.69

Olbas pastilles GSL
Pastille containing eucalyptus oil 1.16% w/w, menthol 0.1% w/w, peppermint oil 1.12% w/w, clove oil 0.002% w/w, juniper-berry oil 0.067% w/w, wintergreen oil 0.047% w/w

Symptomatic relief of colds, coughs, catarrh, sore throats and flu, catarrhal headache and nasal congestion

Children: not suitable for those under 6 years

Price: 45 g £2.05

Robitussin Chesty Cough Medicine PO
Liquid containing in 5 ml guaifenesin 100 mg

Expectorant for treatment of coughs

Children: not recommended for those under 1 year

Price: 100 ml £3.40

continued overleaf

Tixylix Baby Syrup GSL
Sugar-free, colour-free syrup containing in 5 ml glycerol 0.75 ml
For the relief of dry tickly coughs
Children: not recommended for those under 3 months
Price: 100 ml £2.89

Tixylix Chesty Cough GSL
Linctus containing in 5 ml guaifenesin 50 mg
For relief of chesty coughs, hoarseness and sore throats, and to loosen mucus and aid breathing
Children: not recommended for those under 1 year
Price: 100 ml £2.89

Vicks Vaposyrup for Chesty Coughs GSL
Syrup containing in 5 ml guaifenesin 200 mg
For relief of cough, to loosen mucus, soothe and coat the throat and make the cough more productive
Children: not to be given to those under 2 years
Price: 120 ml £2.99

Vicks Vaposyrup for Tickly Coughs GSL
Syrup containing in 10 ml levomenthol 0.125% w/v
Symptomatic relief of dry, irritating cough associated with the common cold
Children: not recommended for those under 6 years
Price: 120 ml £2.99

Herbal preparations

Potter's Chest Mixture GSL
Oral liquid containing in 5 ml horehound liquid extract 0.085 ml, pleurisy root liquid extract 0.05 ml, senega liquid extract 0.06 ml, lobelia acid tincture 0.18 ml, acetum scillae 0.06 ml
A traditional herbal remedy for the symptomatic relief of coughs and catarrh of the upper respiratory tract
Children: not recommended
Price: 150 ml £5.35

Antihistamine-containing cough mixtures

Adult Meltus Night Time P
Syrup containing in 5 ml diphenhydramine hydrochloride 14 mg, ammonium chloride 135 mg, sodium citrate 57 mg

Relief of deep chesty coughs and colds. Makes coughs more productive

Children: dosages given for those aged 6 years and over

Price: 100 ml £3.15

Benylin Chest Coughs (original) P
Syrup containing in 5 ml diphenhydramine hydrochloride 14 mg, levomenthol 2 mg

Relief of cough and associated congestive symptoms

Children: not recommended for those under 6 years

Price: 125 ml £3.39, 300 ml £6.79

Benylin Children's Night Coughs P
Sugar-free and colour-free solution containing in 5 ml diphenhydramine hydrochloride 7 mg, levomenthol 0.55 mg

For relief of cough and its congestive symptoms, and treatment of hay fever and other allergic conditions that affect the upper respiratory tract

Children: not recommended for those under 1 year

Price: 125 ml £3.19

Bronalin expectorant linctus P
Sugar- and colour-free liquid containing in 5 ml ammonium chloride 135 mg, sodium citrate 57 mg, diphenhydramine hydrochloride 14 mg

For symptomatic relief of deep chesty coughs and colds

Children: not recommended for those under 6 years

Price: 100 ml £2.49

Bronalin junior linctus P
Sugar- and colour-free oral liquid containing in 5 ml sodium citrate 28.5 mg, diphenhydramine hydrobromide 7 mg

For the symptomatic relief of coughs and colds, and to reduce irritating coughs and soothe the throat

Children: not recommended for those under 1 year

Price: 100 ml £2.49

continued overleaf

Histalix syrup P

Syrup containing in 5 ml ammonium chloride 135 mg, diphenhydramine hydrochloride 14 mg, menthol 1.1 mg

Symptomatic relief of troublesome cough associated with upper respiratory tract congestion

Children: not to be given to those under 1 year

Price: 150 ml £3.56

Junior Meltus Night-Time P

Syrup containing in 5 ml sodium citrate 28.5 mg, diphenhydramine hydrochloride 7 mg

For relief of coughs and colds, and to reduce irritating coughs and soothe the throat

Children: not recommended for those under 1 year

Price: 100 ml £2.85

Systemic nasal decongestants

Systemic nasal decongestant preparations

Pseudoephedrine hydrochloride

Adult Meltus Expectorant with Decongestant P

Linctus containing in 5 ml guaifenesin 100 mg, pseudoephedrine hydrochloride 30 mg

Symptomatic relief of chesty coughs and congestion associated with colds and influenza

Children: not recommended

Price: 100 ml £3.15

Bronalin Decongestant Elixir P

Sugar- and colour-free liquid containing in 5 ml pseudoephedrine hydrochloride 30 mg

Symptomatic relief of conditions such as the common cold, influenza, hay fever, and allergic and vasomotor rhinitis. Intended for the relief of symptoms such as blocked sinuses, stuffed-up nose and catarrh

Children: not recommended for those under 2 years

Price: 100 ml £2.49

continued opposite

Robitussin Chesty Cough with Congestion P
Liquid containing in 5 ml guaifenesin 100 mg, pseudoephedrine hydrochloride 30 mg
Symptomatic relief of chesty coughs and nasal congestion
Children: not recommended for those under 2 years
Price: 100 ml £3.40

Sudafed expectorant P
Syrup containing in 5 ml guaifenesin 100 mg, pseudoephedrine hydrochloride 30 mg
Symptomatic relief of upper respiratory tract disorders accompanied by productive cough
Children: not recommended for those under 2 years
Price: 100 ml £3.39

Sudafed elixir P
Liquid containing in 5 ml pseudoephedrine hydrochloride 30 mg
Symptomatic relief of allergic rhinits, vasomotor rhinitis, the common cold and influenza
Children: not to be given to those under 2 years
Price: 100 ml £2.45

Sudafed tablets P
Tablet containing pseudoephedrine hydrochloride 60 mg
Symptomatic relief of allergic rhinitis, vasomotor rhinitis, the common cold and influenza
Children: not to be given
Price: 12 £1.99, 24 £3.39

Systemic nasal decongestant/antihistamine preparations

Actifed expectorant P

Liquid containing in 5 ml guaifenesin 100 mg, pseudoephedrine hydrochloride 30 mg, triprolidine hydrochloride 1.25 mg

Symptomatic relief of upper respiratory tract disorders accompanied by productive cough

Children: not recommended for those under 2 years

Price: 100 ml £3.39

Actifed syrup P

Liquid containing in 5 ml pseudoephedrine hydrochloride 30 mg, triprolidine hydrochloride 1.25 mg

Symptomatic relief of upper respiratory tract disorders such as allergic rhinitis, vasomotor rhinitis, the common cold and influenza

Children: not recommended for those under 2 years

Price: 100 ml £3.35

Actifed tablets P

Tablet containing pseudoephedrine hydrochloride 60 mg, triprolidine hydrochloride 2.5 mg

Symptomatic relief of upper respiratory tract disorders such as allergic rhinitis, vasomotor rhinitis, the common cold and influenza

Price: 12 £2.79

Contac 400 P

Capsule containing controlled-release pellets containing chlorpheniramine maleate 4 mg, phenylpropanolamine hydrochloride 50 mg

Relief of nasal congestion and hypersecretion due to colds, hay fever and sinusitis

Children: not recommended

Price: 6 £2.95, 12 £4.79, 24 £6.59

Dimotane expectorant P

Liquid containing in 5 ml guaifenesin 100 mg, pseudoephedrine hydrochloride 30 mg, brompheniramine maleate 2 mg

Symptomatic relief of upper respiratory tract disorders, where an expectorant is also required

Children: not to be used in those under 2 years

Price: 100 ml £3.59

continued opposite

Dimotapp elixir P

Liquid containing in 5 ml phenylephrine hydrochloride 5 mg, phenyl-propanolamine hydrochloride 5 mg, brompheniramine maleate 4 mg

Relief of upper respiratory tract disorders including congestion, hyper-secretion, rhinitis and sinusitis, and helps to relieve hay fever

Children: not to be used in those under 2 years

Price: 100 ml £3.35

Dimotapp elixir paediatric P

Liquid containing in 5 ml phenylephrine hydrochloride 2.5 mg, phenyl-propanolamine hydrochloride 2.5 mg, brompheniramine maleate 1 mg

Treatment of upper respiratory tract disorders, including congestion, hypersecretion, rhinitis and sinusitis, and helps to relieve hay fever

Children: not recommended for those under 2 years

Price: 100 ml £3.19

Dimotapp LA tablets P

Tablet containing phenylephrine hydrochloride 15 mg, phenyl-propanolamine hydrochloride 15 mg, brompheniramine maleate 12 mg

Management of upper respiratory tract disorders including con-gestion, hypersecretion, rhinitis and sinusitis, and symptomatic relief of hay fever

Children: not recommended

Price: 12 £3.89, 24 £6.39, 100 £24.45

Expulin decongestant for babies and children (linctus) P

Liquid containing in 5 ml ephedrine hydrochloride 4 mg, chlor-pheniramine maleate 1 mg

Relief of congestion and runny nose

Children: dosages given for 3 months and older

Price: 100 ml £2.35

continued overleaf

Tixycolds syrup P

Sugar- and colour-free linctus containing in 5 ml diphenhydramine hydrochloride 12.5 mg, pseudoephedrine hydrochloride 22.5 mg

For the relief of symptoms of colds and flu, to relieve stuffy blocked-up nose, dry up a runny nose and help to clear catarrh and blocked sinuses, thus aiding restful sleep

Children: not recommended for those under 1 year

Price: 100 ml £2.89

Triominic tablets P

Tablet containing phenylpropanolamine hydrochloride 25 mg, pheniramine maleate 25 mg

Nasal congestion and allergic rhinitis, including hay fever

Children: not recommended for those under 6 years

Price: 12 £2.55, 30 £4.19

Systemic nasal decongestant/theophylline preparations

Do-Do Chesteze P

Tablet containing caffeine 30 mg, ephedrine hydrochloride 18.31 mg, theophylline anhydrous 100 mg

Relief of bronchial cough, wheezing and breathlessness, and to clear the chest of mucus following upper respiratory tract infection

Children: not recommended for those under 12 years except on medical advice

Price: 12 £1.85, 30 £3.55

Systemic nasal decongestant/aspirin/antihistamine preparations

Dristan decongestant tablets P

Tablet containing caffeine 16.2 mg, phenylephrine hydrochloride 5 mg, aspirin 325 mg, chlorpheniramine maleate 2 mg

Treatment of colds, sinus congestion and catarrh, and for the relief of aches and pains associated with colds and influenza

Children: not recommended except on medical advice

Price: 12 £1.99, 24 £3.49

Systemic nasal decongestant/paracetamol preparations

Anadin Cold Control Capsules GSL
Capsule containing caffeine 25 mg, paracetamol 300 mg, phenylephrine hydrochloride 5 mg
Relief of cold and flu symptoms
Children: should not be given
Price: 16 £2.59

Anadin Cold Control Flu Strength Hot Lemon GSL
Powder containing paracetamol 1000 mg, phenylephrine hydrochloride 10 mg
Relief of symptoms of colds and flu
Children: should not be given
Price: 5 sachets £2.55

Beechams All-In-One GSL
Syrup containing in 20 ml guaifenesin 200 mg, paracetamol 500 mg, phenylephrine hydrochloride 10 mg
Symptomatic relief of colds, chills and influenza
Children: not to be given except on medical advice
Price: 160 ml £3.85

Beechams Cold and Flu Hot Lemon GSL
Sachet of powder containing paracetamol 600 mg, phenylephrine hydrochloride 10 mg, vitamin C 40 mg
Symptomatic relief of symptoms of influenza, feverishness, chills and feverish colds, including headache, sore throat pain, general aches and pains, nasal congestion, sinusitis (and associated pain) and acute nasal catarrh
Children: not to be given except on medical advice
Price: 5 £1.69, 10 £2.69 Blackcurrant, and honey and lemon flavours are also available

Beechams Flu-Plus Caplets GSL
Tablet containing paracetamol 500 mg, caffeine 25 mg, phenylephrine hydrochloride 5 mg
Short-term relief of the symptoms of colds, flu and chills, including headaches, shivers, general aches and pains, congested or blocked nose, painful sinuses and sore throat pain

continued opposite

Children: not recommended except on medical advice

Price: 16 £2.95, 24 £3.99

Beechams Flu-Plus Hot Berry Fruits GSL
Powder containing paracetamol 1000 mg, vitamin C 60 mg, phenyl-ephrine hydrochloride 10 mg

Symptomatic relief of influenza, feverishness, chills and colds includ-ing headache, sore throat pain, aches and pains, nasal congestion, sinusitis (and associated pain) and acute nasal catarrh

Children: not to be given except on medical advice

Price: 5 £2.69 Hot lemon flavour is also available

Beechams Powders Capsules GSL
Capsule containing caffeine 25 mg, paracetamol 300 mg, phenylephrine hydrochloride 5 mg

Symptomatic relief of influenza, feverishness, chills and colds, including feverish colds, as well as nasal congestion and difficult breathing arising from this, sinusitis (and associated pain) and acute nasal catarrh

Children: not recommended for those under 6 years except on medical advice

Price: 10 £1.89, 16 £2.65

Benylin Day and Night P
Daytime tablet containing paracetamol 500 mg, phenylpropanolamine hydrochloride 25 mg

Night-time tablet containing paracetamol 500 mg, diphenhydramine hydrochloride 25 mg

Relief of symptoms associated with colds and influenza

Children: not recommended

Price: 20 £3.79

Catarrh-Ex GSL
Capsule containing caffeine 25 mg, paracetamol 300 mg, phenyl-ephrine hydrochloride 5 mg

Relief of blocked nose, sinus pain and catarrh. Also helps to relieve the symptoms of colds and flu

Children: should not be given

Price: 16 £2.29

continued overleaf

Lemsip Cold + Flu Combined Relief Capsules GSL
Capsule containing paracetamol 300 mg, caffeine 25 mg, phenylephrine hydrochloride 5 mg

Relief of symptoms associated with the common cold and influenza, relief of general aches and pains and nasal congestion, and lowering of temperature

Children: not recommended

Price: 8 £1.59, 16 £2.55

Lemsip Cold + Flu Max Strength GSL
Powder containing paracetamol 1000 mg, vitamin C 100 mg, phenylephrine hydrochloride 12 mg

Symptomatic relief of colds and flu, including aches and pains, nasal congestion and lowering of temperature

Children: not to be given except on medical advice

Price: 5 £2.75, 10 £3.75

Lemsip Cold + Flu Max Strength Capsules GSL
Capsule containing paracetamol 500 mg, caffeine 25 mg, phenylephrine hydrochloride 6.1 mg

Symptomatic relief of colds and flu

Children: should not be given

Price: 8 £1.99, 16 £2.95

Lemsip Cold + Flu Original Lemon GSL
Powder containing paracetamol 650 mg, vitamin C 50 mg, phenylephrine hydrochloride 10 mg

Relief of the symptoms of colds and influenza, including the relief of aches and pains and nasal congestion, and lowering of temperature

Children: should not be given

Price: 5 £1.75, 10 £2.75 Blackcurrant flavour is also available

Breathe Easy pack is also available. Price: 5 £1.99, 10 £3.19

Lemsip Pharmacy Powder + Paracetamol P
Powder containing paracetamol 1000 mg, vitamin C 100 mg, pseudoephedrine hydrochloride 60 mg

Relief of the symptoms of colds and influenza, including relief of aches and pains and nasal congestion, and lowering of temperatue

Children: not to be given except on medical advice

Price: 10 £4.19 *continued opposite*

Mu-Cron tablets P
Tablet containing paracetamol 500 mg, phenylpropanolamine hydro-chloride 25 mg

Relief of sinus pain, nasal congestion and catarrh. Symptomatic relief of nasal congestion caused by hay fever. Symptomatic relief of influenza, feverishness and feverish colds

Children: should not be given

Price: 12 £2.60, 30 £4.29

Paracets Plus Capsules GSL
Capsule containing caffeine 25 mg, paracetamol 300 mg, phenyl-ephrine hydrochloride 5 mg

Relief of symptoms of colds and influenza

Children: should not be given

Price: 16 £1.99

Sinutab tablets P
Tablet containing paracetamol 500 mg, phenylpropanolamine hydro-chloride 12.5 mg

Relief of nasal and sinus congestion and associated headache, sinus pain, fever and congestive symptoms associated with the common cold, influenza and hay fever

Children: not to be given to those under 6 years

Price: 15 £2.99, 30 £4.49

Sudafed Co. tablets P
Tablet containing paracetamol 500 mg, pseudoephedrine hydro-chloride 60 mg

Symptomatic relief of conditions in which upper respiratory congestion is associated with pyrexia and/or pain, including the common cold, influenza, sinusitis and nasopharyngitis

Children: not recommended for those under 6 years

Price: 12 £2.95

Triogesic tablets P
Tablet containing paracetamol 500 mg, phenylpropanolamine hydro-chloride 12.5 mg

Nasal and sinus congestion and associated pain

Children: not recommended for those under 6 years

Price: 12 £2.55, 30 £4.19

Systemic nasal decongestant/paracetamol/antihistamine preparations

Benylin Four Flu hot drink P
Powder containing paracetamol 1000 mg, phenylephrine hydrochloride 12 mg, diphenhydramine hydrochloride 25 mg
Symptomatic relief of colds and flu, including cough, fever, headache, muscular aches and pains and congestion
Children: not suitable
Price: 5 £2.65

Benylin Four Flu liquid P
Tablet containing paracetamol 500 mg, pseudoephedrine hydrochloride 22.5 mg, diphenhydramine hydrochloride 12.5 mg
Relief of symptoms associated with colds and flu, including cough, fever, headache, muscular aches and pains and congestion
Children: not recommended for those under 6 years
Price: 200 ml £4.69

Benylin Four Flu tablets P
Tablet containing paracetamol 500 mg, pseudoephedrine hydrochloride 22.5 mg, diphenhydramine hydrochloride 12.5 mg
Relief of symptoms associated with colds and flu, including cough, fever, headache, muscular aches and pains and congestion
Children: not recommended for those under 6 years
Price: 24 £4.29

Dolvan tablets P
Tablet containing caffeine 30 mg, diphenhydramine hydrochloride 7.5 mg, ephedrine hydrochloride 7.5 mg, paracetamol 300 mg
Relief from symptoms of the common cold and influenza, and of nasal congestion associated with allergic stimuli
Children: not recommended
Price: 20 £4.30

Systemic nasal decongestant/paracetamol/cough suppressant preparations

Day Nurse P

Liquid containing in 20 ml paracetamol 1000 mg, phenylpropanol-amine hydrochloride 25 mg, dextromethorphan hydrobromide 15 mg

Symptomatic relief of colds and influenza, including shivers, aches and pains, blocked or runny nose and tickly cough

Children: not to be given except on medical advice

Price: 160 ml £4.59

Day Nurse capsules P

Capsule containing paracetamol 500 mg, phenylpropanolamine hydrochloride 12.5 mg, dextromethorphan hydrobromide 7.5 mg

Symptomatic relief of colds and influenza, including shivers, aches and pains, blocked or runny nose and tickly cough

Children: not to be given except on medical advice

Price: 20 £3.99

Systemic nasal decongestant/paracetamol/antihistamine/ cough suppressant preparations

Vicks Medinight P

Syrup containing in 30 ml paracetamol 600 mg, dextromethorphan hydrobromide 15 mg, pseudoephedrine hydrochloride 60 mg, doxyl-amine succinate 7.5 mg

Treatment of symptoms of common cold, accompanied by sneezing, headache, body ache, sore throat, cough and nasal congestion

Children: not to be given to those under 10 years

Price: 180 ml £4.49

Systemic nasal decongestant/ibuprofen preparations

Advil Cold and Sinus tablets P

Tablet containing ibuprofen 200 mg, pseudoephedrine hydrochloride 30 mg

Symptomatic relief of nasal and/or sinus congestion with headache, pain, fever and other symptoms of the common cold or influenza

Children: should not be given

Price: 10 £2.39, 20 £3.79

Lemsip Pharmacy Powercaps P

M/R capsule containing ibuprofen 300 mg, pseudoephedrine hydro-chloride 45 mg

Relief of symptoms of heavy cold and influenza, including relief of aches and pains, headache, sore throat and nasal congestion

Children: should not be given

Price: 10 £3.15

Nurofen Cold and Flu P

Tablet containing ibuprofen 200 mg, pseudoephedrine hydrochloride 30 mg

Relief of symptoms of colds and flu with associated congestion, including aches and pains, headache, fever, sore throat, and blocked nose and sinuses

Children: not to be given to those under 12 years

Price: 12 £2.85, 24 £4.45, 36 £5.85

Herbal preparations for congestion

Potter's Catarrh Mixture GSL

Sugar-free liquid containing in 5 ml blue flag liquid extract 0.05 ml, burdock root liquid extract 0.25 ml, boneset liquid extract 0.6 ml, hyssop liquid extract 0.35 ml

A herbal remedy traditionally used for the symptomatic relief of nasal catarrh and catarrh of the throat

Children: not recommended for those under 7 years

Price: 150 ml £7.19

Central nervous system

Hypnotics and anxiolytics

Sedating antihistamines

Diphenhydramine hydrochloride

Nytol P
Caplet containing diphenhydramine hydrochloride 25 mg
An aid to the relief of temporary sleep disturbance
Children: not to be given to those under 16 years
Price: 16 £2.75

Nytol One-A-Night P
Caplet containing diphenhydramine hydrochloride 50 mg
An aid to the relief of temporary sleep disturbance
Children: not to be given to those under 16 years
Price: 16 £4.15

Paxidorm syrup P
Syrup containing in 5 ml diphenhydramine hydrochloride 10 mg
Short-term relief of temporary sleeplessness
Children: not recommended for those under 16 years
Price: 150 ml £3.59

Paxidorm tablets P
Tablet containing diphenhydramine hydrochloride 25 mg
For the relief of temporary sleeplessness
Children: not recommended for those under 16 years
Price: 20 £2.40

Promethazine hydrochloride

Sominex P
Tablet containing promethazine hydrochloride 20 mg
To aid night-time sleep
Children: not recommended for those under 16 years without medical advice
Price: 8 £2.89

Herbal preparations

Hofels Passiflora and Wild Lettuce GSL
Tablet containing passiflora powder 90 mg, wild lettuce extract 18 mg
A herbal remedy to promote natural sleep
Not recommended for children or pregnant or lactating women
Price: 30 £3.99

Hofels Valerian and Gentian GSL
Tablet containing valerian extract 31.45 mg, gentian extract 19 mg, skullcap extract 28 mg
A herbal remedy for the symptomatic relief of tension and stress
Dosage given for adults only
Price: 30 £3.99

Kalms tablets GSL
Tablet containing *Humulus lupulus* powder 45 mg, *Gentiana lutea* powdered extract from 90 mg, *Valeriana officinalis* powdered extract from 135 mg
To relieve periods of worry and irritability, and exogenous stresses and strains, for the relief of worry, wakefulness and other symptoms associated with the menopause, including flushing and cold sweats, and also to promote natural sleep
Children: should not be given
Price: 100 £3.89, 200 £6.75

Natracalm GSL
Tablet containing *Passiflora incarnata* dry extract 500 mg
Traditional herbal remedy for the symptomatic relief of nervous tension and the stresses and strains of everyday life

continued opposite

Children: not recommended
Price: 48 £3.29, 96 £5.19

Natrasleep GSL
Tablet containing *Humulus lupulus* 1. 167 mg, *Valeriana officinalis* 1. 250 mg
Herbal remedy traditionally used to encourage natural sleep
Children: not recommended
Price: 32 £3.29

Nytol Herbal GSL
Tablet containing dogwood jamaica 90 mg, hops 30 mg, passiflora dry extract 5:1 36 mg, wild lettuce dry extract 5:1 54 mg, pulsatilla dry extract 3:1 15 mg
Relief of temporary sleeplessness
Children: should not be given
Price: 28 £4.49

Potter's Newrelax GSL
Tablet containing hops 75 mg, skullcap 45 mg, valerian dry extract 4:1 25 mg, vervain dry extract 3:1 30 mg
A herbal remedy traditionally used for symptomatic relief of tension, irritability or agitation due to the stresses and strains of modern life
Children: not recommended
Price: 50 £2.99, 100 £4.79

Potter's Nodoff Passiflora Tablets GSL
Tablet containing passiflora dry extract 5:1 36 mg
A herbal remedy traditionally used as an aid to promote natural sleep
Children: not recommended
Price: 50 £2.59, 100 £4.75

Seven Seas Slumber Tablets GSL
Tablet containing wild lettuce powder 10 mg, passiflora powder 90 mg, lupulus powder 30 mg, wild lettuce powdered extract 18 mg, piscidia powdered extract 11.25 mg
A traditional herbal remedy to promote natural sleep
Dosage only given for adults and elderly
Price: 60 £3.95

Central nervous system stimulants

Caffeine

Pro-Plus tablets GSL
Tablet containing caffeine 50 mg
Relief of temporary tiredness
Children: should not be given
Price: 24 £2.05, 48 £3.49, 96 £4.99

Yeast-Vite GSL
Tablet containing caffeine 50 mg, vitamin B_1 0.167 mg, vitamin B_{20} 167 mg, nicotinamide 1.75 mg
Relief of fatigue and drowsiness
Children: not to be given except on medical advice
Price: 24 £2.09, 50 £3.35, 100 £4.99

Drugs used in the treatment of obesity

Methylcellulose

Celevac – see section on laxatives

Drugs used in the treatment of nausea and vertigo

Antihistamines

Cinnarizine

Stugeron 15 tablets P
Tablet containing cinnarizine 15 mg
Effective in the control of travel sickness
Children: dosages given for those aged 5 years and over
Price: 15 £2.40

Meclozine hydrochloride

Sea-Legs P

Tablet containing meclozine hydrochloride 12.5 mg

Prevention and treatment of motion sickness

Children: not to be given to those under 2 years

Price: 12 £2.15

Promethazine hydrochloride

Avomine P

Tablet containing promethazine theoclate 25 mg

Prevention and relief of travel sickness and general nausea

Children: dosages given for those aged 5 years and over

Price: 10 £1.95

Hyoscine

Hyoscine hydrobromide

Joy-Rides P

Tablet containing hyoscine hydrobromide 0.15 mg

Prevention of motion sickness

Childrern: not recommended for those under 3 years except on medical advice

Price: 12 £2.15

Junior Kwells P

Tablet containing hyoscine hydrobromide 150µg

Prevention and relief of travel sickness

Children: not recommended for those under 4 years

Price: 12 £2.10

Kwells tablets P

Tablet containing hyoscine hydrobromide 300µg

Prevention of travel sickness

Children: dosages given for those over 10 years

Price: 12 £2.10

Analgesics

Non-opioid analgesics

Aspirin

Aspirin (non-proprietary) P or GSL depending on pack size
Tablet containing aspirin 300 mg

Relief of mild to moderate pain and pyrexia

Children: not to be given to those under 12 years

Price varies

Aspro Clear GSL
Effervescent tablet containing aspirin 300 mg

Relief of influenza, feverishness, feverish colds and lumbago, sciatica, fibrositis, rheumatic pains, and muscular aches and pains. Also relief of mild to moderate pain including headache, migraine, toothache, period pains, sore throat, neuralgia, and general aches and pains

Children: not recommended except on medical advice

Price: 18 £1.79, 30 £2.49

Disprin GSL
Dispersible tablet containing aspirin 300 mg

Relief of mild to moderate pain in headaches (including migraine headaches), toothache, neuralgia, sciatica, period pains and sore throats. Symptomatic relief of feverishness, influenza and colds, rheumatism and lumbago

Children: not to be given except on medical advice

Price: 8 £0.84, 16 £1.35

Disprin Direct GSL
Dispersible tablet containing aspirin 300 mg

Relief of mild to moderate pain in headaches (including tension headaches and migraine headaches), toothache, neuralgia, period pains, rheumatic pain, lumbago and sciatica. Also symptomatic relief of influenza, feverishness, feverish colds and sore throats

Children: not to be given except on medical advice

Price: 16 £1.56

continued opposite

Maximum Strength Aspro Clear GSL
Effervescent tablet containing aspirin 500 mg

Treatment of headaches, migraines, backache, neuralgia, period pains and dental pain. Symptomatic relief of colds, influenza and sore throats, and also reduces temperature. Relief of pain due to strains, sprains, rheumatic pain, lumbago, fibrositis, muscular aches and pains, joint swelling and stiffness

Children: not recommended

Price: 16 £2.09

Aspirin with caffeine and/or low-dose opioid analgesic

Anadin Analgesic Capsules Maximum Strength P
Capsule containing aspirin 500 mg, caffeine 32 mg

Symptomatic relief of influenza and the common cold. Treatment of mild to moderate pain, including headache, migraine, neuralgia, dental pains, period pains, and muscular aches and pains

Children: not recommended except on medical advice

Price: 24 £3.45

Anadin Tablets P or GSL depending on pack size
Tablet containing aspirin 325 mg, caffeine 15 mg

Symptomatic relief of headache, neuralgia, migraine, toothache, sore throat, period pains, general aches and pains, sprains, strains, rheumatic pain, sciatica, lumbago, fibrositis, joint swelling and stiffness, influenza, feverishness and feverish colds

Children: not recommended except on medical advice

Price: 6 £0.75, 12 £1.35, 16 £1.69, 32 £2.55

Beechams Powders P or GSL depending on pack size
Powder containing caffeine 50 mg, aspirin 600 mg

Symptomatic relief of influenza, feverishness, chills, colds and feverish colds. Relief of mild to moderate pain, including headache, migraine, neuralgia, toothache, sore throat, period pains, aches and pains, rheumatic pain and muscular aches and pains

Children: not to be given except on medical advice

Price: 10 £2.25, 20 £3.15

Codis 500 P
Dispersible tablet containing aspirin 500 mg, codeine phosphate 8 mg

Relief of mild to moderate pain, including headache, migraine, neuralgia, toothache, period pains, sprains, strains, rheumatic pain, sciatica, lumbago, fibrositis, muscular aches and pains, joint swelling and stiffness, colds, influenza and feverish conditions

Children: not to be given except on medical advice

Price: 24 £3.25

continued opposite

Phensic Original GSL
Tablet containing aspirin 325 mg, caffeine 22 mg

Symptomatic relief of mild to moderate pain and of minor upper respiratory tract infections

Children: not recommended except on medical advice

Price: 12 £0.95, 24 £1.75

Paracetamol

Paracetamol (non-proprietary) P or GSL depending on pack size
Tablet containing paracetamol 500 mg

For the relief of headache, rheumatic pains, neuralgia and the symptoms of colds and influenza

Children: not recommended in those under 6 years except on medical advice

Price varies

Paracetamol suspension (non-proprietary) P
Suspension containing paracetamol 120 mg/5 ml

Treatment of mild to moderate pain, and also acts as an antipyretic

Children: not to be given to those under 3 months except under medical supervision or following vaccination at 2 months

Price varies

Anadin Paracetamol P or GSL depending on pack size
Tablet containing paracetamol 500 mg

Treatment of headache, migraine, neuralgia, rheumatic pain, period pains, dental pain and the symptoms of colds and influenza

Children: not recommended for those under 6 years except on medical advice

Price: 8 £0.99, 16 £1.69, 32 £2.55

Calpol Infant suspension P
Suspension containing in 5 ml paracetamol 120 mg

Treatment of mild to moderate pain (including teething pain) and as an antipyretic

Children: not to be given to babies under 3 months except under medical supervision or following vaccination at 2 months

Price: 70 ml £1.95, 140 ml £3.49   Sugar-free version is also available

Calpol Infant suspension sachets GSL
Suspension containing in 5 ml paracetamol 120 mg

Treatment of mild to moderate pain (including teething pain) and as an antipyretic

Children: not to be given to babies under 3 months except under medical supervision or following vaccination at 2 months

Price: 10 × 5 ml sachets £2.75   Sugar-free version is also available

continued opposite

Calpol Six Plus suspension P
Suspension containing in 5 ml paracetamol 250 mg

Treatment of mild to moderate pain (including teething pain) and as an antipyretic

Children: not recommended for those under 1 year (or under 6 years for sugar-free version)

Price: 100 ml £3.39 Sugar-free and colour-free version is also available

Disprol Paracetamol suspension P (sachets GSL)
Sugar-free suspension containing in 5 ml paracetamol 120 mg

Mild to moderate pain, including headache, migraine, neuralgia, toothache, teething, sore throat, period pains. Symptomatic relief of rheumatic aches and pains, influenza, feverishness, feverish colds and reactions due to vaccination and immunisation

Children: not to be given to those under 3 months or for longer than 3 days except on medical advice. Can be given to babies who develop fever following vaccination at 2 months

Price: 100 ml £2.35 Sachets 12 × 5 ml £2.79

Disprol Soluble Paracetamol tablets GSL
Effervescent tablet containing paracetamol 120 mg

Treatment of mild to moderate pain, including headache, migraine, neuralgia, toothache, pain in teething, sore throat, and general aches and pains. Symptomatic relief of rheumatic aches and pains, influenza, feverishness and feverish colds

Children: not to be given to those under 1 year or for more than 3 days except on medical advice

Price: 16 £1.35

Fennings Children's Cooling Powders GSL or P depending on pack size
Powder containing paracetamol 50 mg

Pain arising from teething, headache, and general aches and pains. Symptomatic relief of feverish colds, influenza and mild feverish conditions

Children: dosages given for 3 months and over

Price: 10 £1.39, 20 £1.89

continued overleaf

Hedex tablets P or GSL depending on pack size
Tablet containing paracetamol 500 mg

Relief of headaches (including migraine and tension headaches), backache, rheumatic and muscle pain, period pains, nerve pain and toothache, and for relieving the fever, aches and pains of colds and influenza

Children: not to be given to those under 6 years

Price: 16 £1.59, 32 £2.65

Medinol Over 6 Paracetamol oral suspension P
Sugar- and colour-free oral suspension containing in 5 ml paracetamol 250 mg

Mild to moderate pain including headache, migraine, neuralgia, toothache and sore throat. Symptomatic relief of rheumatic aches and pains. Symptomatic relief of influenza, feverishness and colds

Children: not recommended for those under 6 years

Price: 100 ml £2.35, 200 ml £3.70

Medinol Under 6 Paracetamol oral suspension P
Sugar- and colour-free suspension containing in 5 ml paracetamol 120 mg

Relief of pain and feverish conditions

Children: in infants under 3 months only under medical supervision, or in babies who develop a fever following vaccination at 2 months

Price: 70 ml £1.70, 140 ml £3.15

Panadol capsules GSL
Capsule containing paracetamol 500 mg

Relief of headache (including migraine and tension headaches), backache, rheumatic and muscle pains, neuralgia, period pains, toothache, sore throat, and for relieving the fever, aches and pains of colds and influenza

Children: not recommended

Price: 16 £2.05

continued opposite

Panadol Soluble P or GSL depending on pack size
Effervescent tablet containing paracetamol 500 mg

Relief of headache (including migraine and tension headache), toothache, neuralgia, backache, rheumatic and muscle pain, dysmenorrhoea, sore throat, and for relieving the fever, aches and pains of colds and influenza

Children: not to be given to those under 6 years, or to any child for more than 3 days without medical advice

Price: 12 £1.85, 24 £3.19

Panadol tablets P or GSL depending on pack size
Tablet containing paracetamol 500 mg

Relief of headache (including migraine and tension headaches), toothache, backache, rheumatic and muscle pain, neuralgia, sore throat, dysmenorrhoea, and for relieving the fever, aches and pains of colds and influenza. Also for the pain of non-serious arthritis

Children: not to be given to those under 6 years, or to any child for longer than 3 days without medical advice

Price: 12 £1.39, 16 £1.79, 32 £2.99

Paracets capsules GSL
Capsule containing paracetamol 500 mg

Relief of mild to moderate pain, including rheumatic and muscular pain, backache, neuralgia, migraine, headache, toothache and period pains. For the symptomatic relief of feverishness, colds and influenza

Children: should not be given

Price: 16 £1.39

Tixymol P
Suspension containing in 5 ml paracetamol 120 mg

To relieve pain and reduce fever in many conditions, including headache, toothache, teething, feverishness, colds and influenza

Children: in infants under 3 months, only with doctor's advice, or for post-vaccination fever at 2 months

Price: 100 ml £2.15, 150 ml £3.19

Paracetamol with caffeine and/or low-dose opioid analgesic

Co-codamol (non-proprietary) P
Tablet containing paracetamol 500 mg, codeine phosphate 8 mg

For the relief of mild to moderate pain such as headache, period pains, neuralgia, toothache, rheumatic pain and the symptoms of colds and influenza

Children: not recommended for those under 6 years except under medical supervision

Price varies

Boots Dental Pain Relief P
Tablet containing paracetamol 500 mg, dihydrocodeine tartrate 7.46 mg

For the relief of toothache and other dental pain

Children: not recommended

Price: 24 £3.69

Hedex Extra tablets GSL
Tablet containing paracetamol 500 mg, caffeine 65 mg

For the relief of headache (including migraine), toothache, neuralgia, rheumatic pain and dysmenorrhoea, and the relief of symptoms of colds, influenza and sore throat

Children: not recommended except on medical advice

Price: 16 £1.95

Panadol Extra Soluble tablets GSL
Effervescent tablet containing paracetamol 500 mg, caffeine 65 mg

For the relief of headache, backache, and rheumatic and muscle pain, as well as relief of discomfort in colds, influenza and sore throat, and reducing temperature

Children: not recommended except on medical advice

Price: 24 £3.69

Panadol Extra tablets P or GSL depending on pack size
Tablet containing paracetamol 500 mg, caffeine 65 mg

For the relief of headache (including migraine), toothache, neuralgia, rheumatic pain, muscle pain, backache and dysmenorrhoea, the relief

continued opposite

of symptoms of colds, influenza and sore throat, and reducing temperature

Children: not to be given except on medical advice

Price: 12 £1.55, 16 £2.05, 32 £3.49

Panadol Ultra P

Tablet containing paracetamol 500 mg, codeine phosphate hemi-hydrate 12.8 mg

Relief of mild to moderate pain, including migraine, sinusitis, dental pain, arthritic and rheumatic pain, sciatica and lumbago, strains and sprains and dysmenorrhoea. Also for relief of pain and febrile symptoms of colds, sore throats and influenza

Children: should not be given

Price: 20 £3.65

Paracodol capsules P

Capsule containing paracetamol 500 mg, codeine phosphate 8 mg

Treatment of pain, including muscular and rheumatic pains, headache, migraine, neuralgia, toothache, sore throat, period pains, and general aches and pains. Also relief of discomfort associated with influenza, feverishness and feverish colds

Children: should not be given

Price: 10 £1.75, 20 £2.69

Paracodol tablets P

Soluble tablet containing paracetamol 500 mg, codeine phosphate 8 mg

Treatment of pain, including muscular pains, headache, migraine, neuralgia, toothache, sore throat, period pains, and general aches and pains. Also relief of discomfort associated with influenza, feverishness and feverish colds

Children: not recommended for those under 6 years

Price: 12 £2.09, 24 £3.39

Paramol tablets P

Tablet containing paracetamol 500 mg, dihydrocodeine tartrate 7.46 mg

Treatment of mild to moderate pain and as an antipyretic. Has well-defined antitussive activity

Children: should not be given

Price: 12 £2.45, 24 £4.09, 32 £4.65

continued overleaf

Phensic dual action capsules P

Capsule containing paracetamol 500 mg, codeine phosphate 8 mg, caffeine 30 mg

Relief of moderate to strong pain, suitable for migraine, headache, rheumatic pain, period pains, toothache, neuralgia, sore throat, feverishness, colds and influenza

Children: should not be given

Price: 24 £2.69

Solpadeine Max P

Capsule containing paracetamol 500 mg, codeine phosphate hemihydrate 12.8 mg

Relief of mild to moderate pain, including headache, migraine, sinusitis, dental pain, arthritic and rheumatic pain, sciatica and lumbago, strains and sprains and dysmenorrhoea. Also for relief of pain and febrile symptoms of colds, sore throats and influenza

Children: should not be given

Price: 20 £3.85, 30 £4.99

Solpadeine Soluble tablets P

Effervescent tablet containing paracetamol 500 mg, caffeine 30 mg, codeine phosphate 8 mg

Relief of rheumatic pain, headache, migraine, neuralgia, toothache, sore throat, period pains, feverishness and the symptoms of colds and influenza

Children: not to be given to those under 7 years, or to any child for longer than 3 days without medical advice

Price: 12 £2.35, 24 £4.09, 60 £7.35

Solpadeine tablets P

Tablet containing paracetamol 500 mg, caffeine 30 mg, codeine phosphate 8 mg

Pain relief for migraine, headache, rheumatic pain, period pains, toothache, neuralgia, colds, influenza, sore throat and feverishness

Children: should not be given

Price: 6 £0.99, 12 £2.05, 24 £3.79, 32 £4.59   Capsules are also available: 12 £2.15, 24 £3.89, 32 £4.75

Ibuprofen

Ibuprofen (non-proprietary) P or GSL depending on pack size

Tablet containing either 200 mg (GSL or P) or 400 mg (P) ibuprofen

For relief of rheumatic and muscular pain, backache, neuralgia, migraine, headache, dental pain, dysmenorrhea, feverishness, symptoms of colds and influenza

Children: not to be given to those under 12 years

Price varies

Advil tablets P or GSL depending on pack size
Tablet containing ibuprofen 200 mg

Relief of mild to moderate pain, including rheumatic and muscular pain, backache, neuralgia, migraine, headache, dental pain, period pains, feverishness and symptoms of colds and influenza

Children: should not be given except on medical advice

Price: 8 £1.19, 12 £1.65, 24 £2.99, 48 £5.19, 96 £8.85

Advil Tablets Extra Strength P
Tablet containing ibuprofen 400 mg

Relief of mild to moderate pain, including rheumatic and muscular pain, backache, headache, toothache, migraine, neuralgia and period pains, and for relief of symptoms of colds and influenza

Children: should not be given

Price: 24 £5.35, 48 £8.85

Anadin Ibuprofen P or GSL depending on pack size
Tablet containing ibuprofen 200 mg

Relief of mild to moderate pain, including headache, dental pain and period pains, and for the relief of rheumatic and muscular pain, backache and neuralgia

Children: should not be given except on medical advice

Price: 12 £1.45, 16 £1.75, 24 £2.19, 96 £7.25

Anadin Ultra GSL
Capsule containing ibuprofen 200 mg

Relief of mild to moderate pain, including rheumatic and muscular pain, backache, headache, migraine, dental pain, neuralgia,

continued overleaf

Anadin Ultra GSL (*cont.*)
dysmenorrhoea and feverishness, and for the relief of symptoms of colds and influenza. Also for the symptomatic relief of the pain of non-serious arthritic conditions

Children: should not be given

Price: 4 75p, 16 £2.59

Cuprofen Ibuprofen tablets P
Tablet containing ibuprofen 200 mg

Relief of rheumatic, muscular, dental and period pains, backache, lumbago, fibrositis, neuralgia, migraine and headache, and for symptomatic relief of colds, influenza and feverishness

Children: not recommended

Price: 12 £0.99, 24 £1.25, 48 £2.25, 96 £3.99

Cuprofen Tablets Maximum Strength P
Tablet containing ibuprofen 400 mg

Rheumatic, muscular, dental and period pains, and pain in backache, lumbago, fibrositis, neuralgia, migraine and headache, and for symptomatic relief of colds, influenza and feverishness

Children: should not be given

Price: 12 £1.45, 24 £2.25, 48 £3.99, 96 £6.99

Hedex Ibuprofen tablets GSL
Tablet containing 200 mg ibuprofen

Relief of headache, including tension headaches and migraine. Also for relief of rheumatic and muscular pains, period pains, backache, neuralgia, toothache, feverishness and symptoms of colds and influenza

Children: should not be given

Price: 12 £1.55

Nurofen P or GSL depending on pack size
Tablet containing ibuprofen 200 mg

Relief of headaches, cold and influenza symptoms, rheumatic pain, muscular pain, backache, feverishness, migraine, period pains, dental pain and neuralgia

Children: should not be given except under medical advice

Price: 12 £1.69, 16 £2.25, 24 £3.05, 48 £5.59, 96 £9.19   Caplets are also available: 12 £1.79, 16 £2.35

continued opposite

Nurofen Advance P

Tablet containing ibuprofen lysine 342 mg

Relief of mild to moderate pain including headache, backache, period pains, dental pain, neuralgia, rheumatic pain, muscular pain, migraine, cold and influenza symptoms and feverishness

Children: should not be given

Price: 10 £1.85, 20 £3.25, 40 £6.09

Nurofen for Children (sugar-free) P

Sugar-free and colour-free suspension containing in 5 ml ibuprofen 100 mg

For fast and effective reduction of fever, including post-immunisation pyrexia, and fast and effective relief of mild to moderate pain, including sore throat, teething pain, toothache, earache, headache, and minor aches and sprains

Children: dosages given from 6 months. For post-immunisation fever, should only be given under medical advice

Price: 100 ml £3.25, 150 ml £4.89

Nurofen Liquid Capsules GSL

Capsule containing ibuprofen 200 mg

For the relief of mild to moderate pain, including headache, backache, period pains, dental pain, neuralgia, rheumatic and muscular pains, migraine, cold and influenza symptoms and feverishness

Children: should not be given except under medical advice

Price: 10 £1.79

Nurofen Long Lasting P

S/R capsule containing ibuprofen 300 mg

Long-lasting relief of backache, dysmenorrhoea, dental pain, non-serious arthritic and rheumatic pain, neuralgia and muscular pains. Also suitable for headache and migraine

Children: should not be given

Price: 12 £2.75, 24 £5.09

continued overleaf

Pacifene P or GSL depending on pack size
Tablet containing ibuprofen 200 mg

Relief of rheumatic and muscular pain, backache, neuralgia, headache, dental pain, migraine, period pains and symptoms of colds and influenza

Children: should not be given

Price: 12 £0.69, 24 £1.25, 48 £2.25, 96 £3.70

Pacifene Maximum Strength P
Tablet containing ibuprofen 400 mg

Treatment of rheumatic and muscular pain, backache, neuralgia, headache, dental pain, migraine, period pains and symptoms of colds and influenza

Children: should not be given

Price: 12 £1.25, 24 £2.25, 48 £3.70

Phensic Ibuprofen P
Tablet containing ibuprofen 200 mg

Relief of headaches, migraine, dental pain, period pains, rheumatic pain, muscular pain, backache, feverishness and neuralgia

Children: should not be given except on medical advice

Price: 24 £1.85

Relcofen 200 mg P
Tablet containing ibuprofen 200 mg or 400 mg

Relief of rheumatic and muscular pain, backache, migraine, headache, period pains, neuralgia, dental pain, feverishness, symptoms of colds and influenza

Children: should not be given

Price: 24 × 200 mg £1.55, 24 × 400 mg £2.38

Ibuprofen with caffeine and/or low-dose opioid analgesic

Nurofen Plus P

Tablet containing ibuprofen 200 mg, codeine phosphate 12.8 mg

Relief of migraine, tension headache, dental pain, cramping period pains, neuralgia, sciatica, lumbago and rheumatic pain

Children: should not be given

Price: 12 £2.39, 24 £4.49, 48 £7.89, 72 £9.99

Solpaflex tablets P

Tablet containing ibuprofen 200 mg, codeine phosphate hemihydrate 12.8 mg

Relief of mild to moderate pain, including rheumatic and muscular pain, backache, neuralgia, migraine, headache, dental pain, dysmenorrhoea, feverishness and symptoms of colds and influenza

Children: not recommended

Price: 12 £1.99, 24 £3.65

Other analgesic preparations:

Alka-Seltzer Original GSL
Effervescent tablet containing sodium bicarbonate 1625 mg, citric acid (anhydrous) 965 mg, aspirin 324 mg

For headache with upset stomach, and relief of mild to moderate pain, including headache, neuralgia, migraine, toothache, sore throat, period pains, general aches and pains, symptomatic relief of sprains and strains, rheumatic pain, sciatica, lumbago, fibrositis, and muscular aches and pains

Children: not recommended except on medical advice

Price: 10 £2.19, 20 £3.49

Alka-Seltzer XS GSL
Effervescent tablet containing aspirin 267 mg, paracetamol 133 mg, sodium bicarbonate 1.606 g, citric acid (anhydrous) 954 mg, caffeine 40 mg

For headache with upset stomach (e.g. hangover) and also general pain relief

Children: not recommended except on medical advice

Price: 10 £2.19, 20 £3.49

Anadin Extra tablets P or GSL depending on pack size
Tablet containing aspirin 300 mg, paracetamol 200 mg, caffeine 45 mg

Symptomatic relief of mild to moderate pain, including headache, migraine, neuralgia, toothache, sore throat, period pains, sprains and strains, rheumatic pain, sciatica, lumbago, fibrositis, muscular aches and pains, joint swelling and stiffness, and symptoms of colds and influenza

Children: not recommended except on medical advice

Price: 8 £1.19, 12 £1.69, 16 £2.09, 32 £3.19

Anadin Extra Soluble tablets GSL
Soluble tablet containing aspirin 300 mg, paracetamol 200 mg, caffeine 45 mg

Symptomatic relief of mild to moderate pain, including headache, migraine, neuralgia, toothache, sore throat, period pains, also symptomatic relief of sprains and strains, rheumatic pain, sciatica, lumbago,

continued opposite

fibrositis, muscular aches and pains, joint swelling and stiffness, and symptoms of cold and influenza

Children: not recommended except on medical advice

Price: 8 £1.49, 16 £2.45

Askit Powders GSL
Powder containing aspirin 530 mg, aloxiprin 140 mg, caffeine 110 mg

Relief of mild to moderate pain, including headache, migraine, neuralgia, toothache, sore throat, period pains, influenza, feverishness, feverish colds, rheumatic pain, backache, sciatica, lumbago, fibrositis, muscular aches and pains, joint swelling and stiffness

Children: not recommended except on medical advice

Price: 4 £0.80, 8 £1.58

Beechams Lemon Tablets GSL
Tablet containing aspirin 300 mg, glycine 150 mg

Symptomatic relief of influenza, feverishness, chills, colds and feverish colds, and relief of mild to moderate pain, including headache, migraine, neuralgia, toothache, sore throat, period pains, rheumatic pain, and muscular aches and pains

Children: should not be given except on medical advice

Price: 16 £1.75

Boots Tension Headache Relief tablets P
Tablet containing paracetamol 450 mg, caffeine 30 mg, codeine phosphate 10 mg, doxylamine succinate 5 mg

Relief of tension headaches

Children: not recommended

Price 24 £3.15

Disprin Extra GSL
Dispersible tablet containing aspirin 300 mg, paracetamol 200 mg

Treatment of mild to moderate pain, including headache, migraine, neuralgia, toothache, sore throat, and muscular aches and pains. Symptomatic relief of rheumatic aches and pains, and relief of influenza, feverishness and feverish colds

Children: should not be given except on medical advice

Price: 16 £1.60

continued overleaf

Feminax P
Tablet containing caffeine 50 mg, paracetamol 500 mg, codeine phosphate 8 mg, hyoscine hydrobromide 0.1 mg
Relief of period pain
Children: not recommended
Price: 20 £2.79

Jackson's Febrifuge GSL
Liquid containing in 5 ml sodium salicylate 0.5g
Symptomatic relief of influenza, sore throat, feverish colds, general muscular aches, strains and sprains, rheumatism, lumbago and fibrositis
Children: should not to be given
Price: 100 ml £1.69

Medised P
Suspension containing in 5 ml paracetamol 120 mg, promethazine hydrochloride 1.5 mg
Relief of mild to moderate pain, including headache, toothache, sore throat, and muscular aches and pains. Symptomatic relief of influenza, feverishness, feverish colds and chicken-pox. Also used for the reduction of nasal irritation and watery discharge
Children: not to be given to those under 1 year except on medical advice
Price: 140 ml £3.55   A sugar-free and colour-free version is available

Medised Infant P
Suspension containing in 5 ml paracetamol 120 mg, diphenhydramine hydrochloride 12.5 mg
Relief of mild to moderate pain, including teething pain, headache, sore throat, and general aches and pains. Symptomatic relief of influenza, feverishness, feverish colds and chicken-pox. Also controls excessive mucous secretion and eases nasal irritation
Children: should not be given to those under 3 months except on medical advice
Price: 100 ml £3.15

Night Nurse P
Syrup containing in 20 ml paracetamol 1000 mg, promethazine hydrochloride 20 mg, dextromethorphan hydrobromide 15 mg

continued opposite

Symptomatic night-time relief of colds, chills and influenza

Children: not recommended for those under 6 years except on medical advice

Price: 160 ml £4.59

Night Nurse Capsules P
Capsule containing paracetamol 500 mg, promethazine hydrochloride 10 mg, dextromethorphan hydrobromide 7.5 mg

Symptomatic night-time relief of colds, chills and influenza

Not recommended for those under 6 years except on medical advice

Price: 10 £3.05

Nurse Sykes' Powders P or GSL depending on pack size
Powder containing aspirin 165.3 mg, paracetamol 120 mg, caffeine 60 mg

Relief of mild to moderate pain, and symptomatic relief of rheumatic aches and pains and fibrositis, as well as influenza, feverishness and feverish colds

Children: not recommended except on medical advice

Price: 8 £1.79, 32 £4.49

Panadol Night P
Capsule containing paracetamol 500 mg, diphenhydramine hydro-chloride 25 mg

For short-term treatment of night-time pain, including rheumatic and muscle pain, backache, neuralgia, toothache, migraine, headache and period pains which are causing difficulty in getting to sleep

Children: not recommended except on medical advice

Price: 10 £2.20, 20 £3.65

Paracets Cold Relief Powders GSL
Powder containing paracetamol 650 mg, vitamin C 50 mg

Relief of cold and influenza symptoms

Children: should not be given

Price: 5 £1.45

Propain tablets P
Tablet containing paracetamol 400 mg, caffeine 50 mg, codeine phosphate 10 mg, diphenhydramine hydrochloride 5 mg

continued overleaf

Propain tablets P (*cont.*)

Relief of headache, migraine, muscular pain, period pains and toothache. Symptomatic relief of influenza, feverishness and colds

Children: should not be given

Price: 12 £2.35, 24 £4.15

Resolve GSL

Sachet of effervescent granules containing paracetamol 1000 mg, vitamin C 30 mg, sodium bicarbonate 808 mg, citric acid (anhydrous) 1185 mg, sodium carbonate (anhydrous) 153 mg, potassium bicarbonate 715 mg

Relief of headache with gastric upset, particularly associated with over-indulgence in food or drink, or both. Also for relief of headache and nausea associated with migraine

Children: not recommended

Price: 5 £2.09, 10 £3.35

Syndol P

Tablet containing paracetamol 450 mg, caffeine 30 mg, codeine phosphate 10 mg, doxylamine succinate 5 mg

Relief of mild to moderate pain headache (muscle-contraction or tension headache), migraine, neuralgia, toothache, sore throat, dysmenorrhoea, muscular and rheumatic pains, and pain following surgical or dental procedures

Children: not recommended

Price: 10 £2.09, 20 £3.35, 30 £4.40

Veganin tablets P

Tablet containing paracetamol 250 mg, aspirin 250 mg, codeine phosphate 6.8 mg

Analgesic and antipyretic for influenza and relief of mild to moderate pain, including headache, dysmenorrhoea, rheumatism and toothache

Price: 10 £1.85, 30 £4.49

Anti-migraine drugs

Analgesics with vasoconstrictor for migraine

Midrid P

Capsule containing paracetamol 325 mg, isometheptane mucate 65 mg

For relief of migraine and throbbing headache

Children: adult dosages only given

Price: 15 £4.25

Analgesics with anti-emetic for migraine

Migraleve P

Pink tablet containing paracetamol 500 mg, codeine phosphate 8 mg, buclizine hydrochloride 6.25 mg

Yellow tablet containing paracetamol 500 mg, codeine phosphate 8 mg

Relief of migraine including headache, nausea and vomiting

Children: not recommended for those under 10 years except under medical supervision

Price: 12 £3.89, 24 £6.85 Migraleve Pink 12 £4.05, 24 £7.55; Migraleve Yellow 12 £3.49, 24 £5.99

Drugs used in substance dependence

Nicotine products

Nicorette Gum 2 mg, 4 mg P
Chewing gum containing nicotine 2 mg or 4 mg

Relief of nicotine withdrawal symptoms as an aid to smoking cessation

Children: not to be used by those under 18 years

Price: 2 mg 15 £2.99, 30 £5.69, 105 £15.59; 4 mg 15 £3.69, 30 £6.99, 105 £18.99 Mint flavour is also available

Nicorette Inhalator P
Inhalation cartridge for oromucosal use containing nicotine 10 mg

Treatment of nicotine dependence, and for the relief of withdrawal symptoms associated with smoking cessation

Children: not to be used by those under 18 years

Price: 6 £5.95, 42 £19.95

Nicorette Microtab P
Sublingual tablet containing nicotine 2 mg

To help smokers who want to give up smoking, but who experience difficulty in doing so due to their nicotine dependence

Children: not to be used by those under 18 years

Price: 30 £6.25, 105 £17.25

Nicorette patch 15 mg, 10 mg, 5 mg P
Transdermal delivery system available in sizes 30, 20 and 10 cm^2, containing nicotine 0.83 mg/cm^2

Treatment of nicotine dependence, and relief of withdrawal symptoms associated with smoking cessation

Children: not to be used by those under 18 years

Price: 15 mg 7 £15.99, 10 mg 7 £14.73, 5 mg 7 £12.69

Nicotinell Fruit Chewing Gum 2 mg, 4 mg P
Chewing gum containing 2 mg or 4 mg nicotine

Relief of nicotine withdrawal symptoms in nicotine dependency as an aid to smoking cessation

Children: should not be used

continued opposite

Price: 2 mg 12 £2.55, 48 £8.99, 96 £14.49; 4 mg 12 £2.75, 48 £9.99, 96 £17.99 Mint flavour is also available

Nicotinell Mint 1 mg lozenges P
Lozenge containing nicotine 1 mg

Relief of nicotine withdrawal symptoms in nicotine dependency as an aid to smoking cessation

Children: not to be used by those under 18 years except under medical supervision

Price: 12 £2.99, 36 £7.49, 96 £15.99

Nicotinell TTS P
Self-adhesive patch containing nicotine 1.75 mg/cm^2

Treatment of nicotine dependence as an aid to smoking cessation

Children: not to be used by those under 18 years

Price: TTS30 2 £4.99, 7 £17.49, 21 £42.99; TTS20 2 £4.50, 7 £16.49; TTS10 7 £15.99

Niquitin CQ 21 mg, 14 mg, 7 mg P
Transdermal patch delivering 21 mg, 14 mg or 7 mg nicotine per 24 hours

Relief of nicotine withdrawal symptoms, including craving, associated with smoking cessation

Children: should not be used

Price: 21 mg 14 £35.95 All strengths, 7 pack £19.95

Infections

Antifungal drugs

Fluconazole

Diflucan One P

Capsule containing fluconazole 150 mg

Oral treatment for vaginal thrush

Adults over 60 years and children: not recommended

Price: 1 £12.50

Antiprotozoal drugs

Antimalarials

Chloroquine

Avloclor tablets P
Tablet containing chloroquine phosphate 250 mg (equivalent to chloroquine base 155 mg)
For the prevention of malaria
Price: 20 £1.96

Malarivon syrup P
Syrup containing in 5 ml chloroquine phosphate 80 mg
For the prevention of malaria
Price: 75 ml £3.35

Nivaquine syrup P
Syrup containing in 5 ml chloroquine sulphate 68 mg (equivalent to chloroquine base 50 mg)
For the prevention of malaria
Price: 100 ml £4.95

Nivaquine tablets P
Tablet containing chloroquine sulphate 200 mg (equivalent to chloroquine base 150 mg)
For the prevention of malaria
Price: 28 £2.35

Proguanil hydrochloride

Paludrine P
Tablet containing proguanil hydrochloride 100 mg
For the prevention of malaria
Price: 98 £13.10 Travel pack: 98 Paludrine + 14 Avloclor £15.50

Anthelmintics

Mebendazole

Ovex tablets P

Orange-flavoured tablet containing mebendazole 100 mg

Treatment of *Enterobius vermicularis* (threadworm)

Children: not to be given to those under 2 years

Price: 1 £1.99, 4 £5.99

Pripsen Mebendazole tablets P

Tablet containing mebendazole 100 mg

Treatment of threadworm (enterobiasis) infestation

Children: not recommended for those under 2 years

Price: 2 £1.99, 8 £5.99

Piperazine

Pripsen Piperazine Citrate Elixir P

Liquid containing in 5 ml piperazine citrate 750 mg

To expel threadworms and roundworms from the gastrointestinal tract

Children: not recommended for those under 1 year except on medical advice

Price: 140 ml £3.39

Pripsen Piperazine Phosphate Powder P

Powder containing piperazine phosphate 4 g, senna standardised 15.3 mg

Eradication of pinworm, threadworm and roundworm

Children: not recommended for those aged 3 months to 1 year, except on medical advice

Price: dual dose pack £2.29

Obstetrics, gynaecology and urinary-tract disorders

Treatment of vaginal and vulval conditions

Non-hormonal preparations for vaginal atrophy

Feminesse GSL

Intravaginal gel with applicator delivering 1.5 g gel containing water purified 78.82% w/w

For vaginal odour

Adult dosage given

Price: 35 g £9.85 Pre-filled applicators 2 £2.75, 8 £9.85

Replens GSL

Intravaginal gel with applicator delivering 2.5 g gel containing water purified 78.82% w/w

Symptomatic relief of vaginal dryness, itching, irritation and coital discomfort in post-menopausal women

Price: 3 £4.29, 6 £7.49

Preparations for vaginal and vulval candidiasis

Clotrimazole

Candiden Cream – *see* section on skin

Candiden Vaginal Tablet P
Tablet containing clotrimazole 500 mg
Treatment of vaginal thrush
Children: should not be used
Price: 1 £5.45

Canesten Cream – *see* section on skin

Canesten Once P
Vaginal cream containing clotrimazole 0.5 g
Treatment of candidal vaginitis
Adults over 60 years and children: not recommended except on medical advice
Price: 5 g £7.89

Canesten Pessary P
Pessary containing clotrimazole 500 mg
Treatment of vaginal candidiasis
Adults over 60 years and children: not recommended except on medical advice
Price: 1 £6.15 Canesten Combi with 20 g cream (1%) £7.89

Canesten Thrush Cream P
Cream containing clotrimazole 2% w/w
Treatment of candidal vulvitis. Should be used as an adjunct to treatment of candidal vaginitis
Children: not recommended
Price: 20 g £4.49

Econazole

Ecostatin Cream – see section on skin

Gyno-Pevaryl 1 P
Polysaccharide-based pessary containing econazole nitrate 150 mg
Treatment of candidal vaginitis
Children: not applicable
Price: 1 £5.94 Gyno-Pevaryl 1 Combipack with 15 g cream £7.67

Gyno-Pevaryl cream P
Cream containing econazole nitrate 1%
Treatment of mycotic vulvovaginitis, mycotic balanitis
Children: not applicable
Price: 15 g £2.64

Gyno-Pevaryl pessaries P
Pessary containing econazole nitrate 150 mg
Treatment of candidal vaginitis
Children: not applicable
Price: 3 £5.59 Gyno-Pevaryl Combipack with 15 g cream £7.67

Miconazole

Daktarin cream – see section on skin

Preparations for other vaginal infections

Aci-Jel GSL
Jelly containing acetic acid 0.94%

Treatment of non-specific chronic vaginitis when an increase in vaginal acidity is appropriate

Children: not applicable

Price: 85 g £5.95

Betadine pessary P
Pessary containing povidone–iodine 200 mg

Treatment of candidal, trichomonal and non-specific vaginitis

Children: not applicable

Price: 28 £10.65

Betadine Vaginal Gel GSL
Gel containing povidone–iodine 10%

Treatment of candidal, trichomonal and non-specific vaginitis

Children: not applicable

Price: 80 g £4.90

Betadine VC kit GSL
Povidone–iodine 10% solution for dilution to cleanser

Treatment of candidal, trichomonal and non-specific vaginitis

Price: 250 ml £4.90

Contraceptives

Spermicidal contraceptives

Delfen GSL
Foam containing nonoxynol-9 12.5%
For use with barrier contraceptives
Price: 20 g £8.20

Double-Check GSL
Pessary containing nonoxynol-9 6%
For use with barrier contraceptives
Price: 10 £1.90

Durex Duragel GSL
Vaginal gel containing nonoxynol-9 2% w/w
For use with barrier contraceptives
Price: 100 g £5.89

Gynol II GSL
Jelly containing nonoxynol-9 2%
For use with diaphragm
Price: 81 g £4.60

Ortho-Creme GSL
Cream containing nonoxynol-9 2%
For use alone or with diaphragm
Price: 70 g £4.30 Applicator £1.32

Ortho-Forms GSL
Pessary containing nonoxynol-9 5%
For use alone or with barrier contraceptives
Price: 15 £4.23

Drugs for genito-urinary disorders

Drugs used for urological pain

Sodium citrate

Canesten Oasis GSL
Effervescent powder providing the equivalent of 4.4 g of sodium citrate

Relief of symptoms of cystitis in women

Not recommended for men or children

Price: 6 £4.25

Cymalon GSL
Granules providing a combined alkalinity equivalent to 4.4 g sodium citrate

Relief of cystitis in adult females only

Children: not recommended

Price: 6 £4.25

Cystoleve Powders GSL
Powder containing sodium citrate 4 g

Relief of symptoms of cystitis in women

Not to be taken by men or children except on medical advice

Price: 6 £4.15

Potassium citrate

Cystopurin GSL
Powder containing potassium citrate 3 g

Relief of the symptoms of cystitis

Children: not recommended for those under 6 years

Price: 6 × 7 g £4.35

Nutrition and blood

Oral rehydration therapy

Dioralyte Natural P

Powder containing glucose anhydrous 3.56 g, sodium chloride 0.47 g, potassium chloride 0.3 g, disodium hydrogen citrate 0.53 g

Correction of fluid and electrolyte loss in infants, children and adults

Children: should only be given to infants under medical supervision

Price: 6 £3.09 Also available in blackcurrant and citrus flavours

Dioralyte Relief Rasberry P

Powder containing sodium chloride 350 mg, potassium chloride 300 mg, sodium citrate 580 mg, pre-cooked rice powder 6 g

Correction of fluid and electrolyte loss in infants aged 3 months or over, children and adults. For infants aged 3 months to 1 year, only use under medical advice

Price: 6 £3.49 Also available in blackcurrant and apricot flavours

Dioralyte Tablets Blackcurrant Flavour P

Effervescent tablet containing sodium bicarbonate 0.336 g, citric acid (anhydrous) 0.384 g, glucose anhydrous 1.62 g, sodium chloride 0.117 g, potassium chloride 0.186 g

Correction of fluid and electrolyte loss in infants, children and adults. Management of mild to moderate dehydration, particularly in acute diarrhoea

Infants: should only be given under medical supervision

Price: 10 £2.49 Also available in citrus flavour

Musculoskeletal and joint diseases

Drugs used in rheumatic disease

Aspirin – *see* section on analgesics

Ibuprofen – *see* section on analgesics

Drugs used for the relief of soft-tissue inflammation

Topical NSAIDs and counter-irritants

Felbinac

Traxam Pain Relief Gel P
Gel containing felbinac 3% w/w
Symptomatic relief of sprains, strains and bruises
Children: should not be used
Price: 30 g £4.29

Ibuprofen

Boots Ibuprofen Gel GSL
Gel containing ibuprofen 5% w/w

For the rapid symptomatic relief of superficial musculoskeletal disorders including backache, rheumatic pains, muscular pains, sprains, strains, lumbago and fibrositis

Children: not recommended for those under 14 years of age

Price: 35 g £3.59

Deep Relief P
Gel containing ibuprofen 5% w/w, levomenthol 3% w/w

Relief of rheumatic pain, and muscular aches, pains and swellings such as strains, sprains and sports injuries. Relief of pain associated with non-serious arthritic conditions

Children: not recommended

Price: 30 g £3.89, 50 g £4.99, 50 g pump £4.99

Ibuleve Gel P
Gel containing ibuprofen 5% w/w

Relief of backache, rheumatic and muscular pain, sprains and strains. Reduces swelling and inflammation. Also for pain relief in common arthritic conditions

Children: not to be used for those under 12 years

Price: 30 g £3.89, 50 g £5.39 Also available as mousse 75 g £7.95, 125 g £10.60 and spray 35 ml £4.75

Ibutop Cuprofen Ibuprofen Gel P (*Ralgex* GSL)
Gel containing ibuprofen 5% w/w

Relief of rheumatic pain, pain due to non-serious arthritic conditions and muscular aches, pains and swellings such as strains, sprains and sports injuries

Children: not to be used except on medical advice

Price: 30 g £3.19, 50 g £4.49 Also Ibutop Ralgex Ibuprofen Gel 30 g £3.75

continued overleaf

Mentholatum Ibuprofen Gel GSL
Gel containing ibuprofen 5% w/w

Symptomatic relief of superficial musculoskeletal disorders, including backache, rheumatic pains, muscular pains, sprains, strains, lumbago and fibrositis

Children: directions given for those aged 14 years and over

Price: 35 g £3.19, 50 g £4.19

Nurofen Muscular Pain Relief Gel GSL
Gel containing ibuprofen 5% w/w

Relief of pain and inflammation in conditions such as backache, rheumatic pains, muscular pains, sprains, strains, lumbago and fibrositis

Children: directions given for those aged 14 years and over

Price: 35 g £4.39

Proflex Pain Relief P
Cream containing ibuprofen 5% w/w

Relief of symptoms of rheumatic and muscular pain, backache, sprains, strains, lumbago, fibrositis and sports injuries

Children: not recommended

Price: 30 g £4.05

Radian B Ibuprofen Gel GSL
Gel containing ibuprofen 5% w/w

Topical analgesic and anti-inflammatory for backache, rheumatic and muscular pain, sprains, strains and neuralgia

Children: not to be used for those under 14 years without medical advice

Price: 30 g £3.99

Piroxicam

Feldene P Gel P
Gel containing piroxicam 0.5% w/w

Relief of the pain of mild arthritis, rheumatism, injured joints, sprains, back strain, fibrositis and tennis elbow

Children: should not be used

Price: 7.5 g £0.99, 30 g £4.39

Other topical NSAIDs and counter-irritants

Algipan Rub GSL

Cream containing glycol salicylate 10% w/w, methyl nicotinate 1% w/w, capsicum oleoresin 0.1% w/w

Symptomatic relief of muscular pain and stiffness in conditions such as backache, sciatica, lumbago, fibrositis and rheumatic pain

Children: not recommended

Price: 40 g £1.99

Balmosa Cream GSL

Cream containing camphor 4% w/w, methyl salicylate 4% w/w, capsicum oleoresin 0.035% w/w

Relief of pain due to unbroken chilblains and muscular rheumatism, fibrositis, lumbago and sciatica

Price: 40 g £1.19

Boots Medicated Pain Relief Plaster GSL

Plaster containing camphor 46.8 mg, levomenthol 37.44 mg, methyl salicylate 74.66 mg

Temporary relief of backache, muscular aches and pains, sprains and strains

Children: not recommended for those under 14 years

Price: 5 £3.79

Chymol Emollient Balm GSL

Ointment containing eucalyptus oil 1.2% w/w, terpineol 4% w/w, methyl salicylate 0.8% w/w, phenol 2.4% w/w

Relief of pain due to chapped and sore skin, chilblains, bruises and sprains

Price: 40 g £2.49

Cuxson Gerrard Belladonna Plaster BP P

Plaster containing belladonna alkaloids 0.25% w/w

A remedy traditionally used for relief of aches and pains, including stiffness, strains, lumbago, rheumatism and sciatica

Not to be used by children under 10 years of age, people with glaucoma, pregnant women or nursing mothers

continued overleaf

Cuxson Gerrard Belladonna Plaster BP P (*cont.*)
Price: White cloth 19 × 12.5 cm £1.29, 28 × 17.5 cm £2.23 Red
flannelette 19 × 12.5 cm £1.61, 28 × 17.5 cm £2.75

Deep Freeze Cold Gel GSL
Gel containing menthol 2% w/w
Symptomatic relief of painful lesions of the muscles, tendons and
joints
Children: not recommended for those under 5 years
Price: 35 g £1.95, 100 g £3.79

Deep Freeze Spray GSL
Aerosol spray containing menthol 2% w/w, *N*-pentane 40% w/w
Symptomatic relief of muscular pain and stiffness, lumbago, sciatica,
fibrositis, sprains, bruises, cramp, and rheumatic pain
Children: not recommended for those under 6 years
Price: 200 ml £3.25

Deep Heat Massage Liniment GSL
Liquid emulsion containing menthol 1.58% w/w, methyl salicylate
18.94% w/w
Symptomatic relief of muscular pain and stiffness, including back-
ache, sciatica, lumbago, fibrositis, rheumatic pain and cramp
Children: not to be used for those under 5 years
Price: 120 ml £4.09

Deep Heat Maximum Strength GSL
Cream emulsion containing menthol 8% w/w, methyl salicylate
30% w/w
Symptomatic relief of muscular pain and stiffness, including back-
ache, sciatica, lumbago, fibrositis, rheumatic pain, bruises and sprains
Children: not to be used for those under 5 years
Price: 30 g £3.75

Deep Heat Rub GSL
Emulsion cream containing turpentine oil 1.47% w/w, eucalyptus oil
1.97% w/w, menthol 5.91% w/w, methyl salicylate 12.8% w/w

continued opposite

Symptomatic relief of muscular pain and stiffness, including back-ache, sciatica, lumbago, fibrositis, rheumatic pain, bruises, sprains and chilblains

Children: not recommended for those under 5 years

Price: standard £2.05, medium £3.09, large £4.09

Deep Heat Spray GSL
Aerosol spray containing methyl salicylate 1% w/w, methyl nicotinate 1.6% w/w, ethyl salicylate 5% w/w, 2-hydroxyethyl salicylate 5% w/w

Symptomatic relief of muscular pain, bursitis and tendinitis, including rheumatic pain, strains, fibrositis, lumbago and sciatica

Children: not to be used for those under 5 years

Price: 150 ml £3.25

Dubam Cream GSL
Cream containing per 100 g methyl salicylate 20 g, menthol 2 g, cineole 1 g

Symptomatic relief of the pain and stiffness associated with muscular rheumatism, lumbago, sciatica, fibrositis, sprains and chilblains

Children: not to be used for those under 6 years

Price: 30 g £2.64 Spray also available £5.94

Elliman's Universal Embrocation GSL
Embrocation containing turpentine oil 35.41% v/v, acetic acid (33%) 10.37% v/v

Symptomatic relief of muscular pain and stiffness, including back-ache, sciatica, lumbago, fibrositis and rheumatic pain

Children: not recommended

Price: 100 ml £2.85

Goddard's Embrocation GSL
Emulsion containing turpentine oil 22% v/v, acetic acid (33%) 30% v/v, ammonia solution dilute 14% v/v

Symptomatic relief of muscular pain and stiffness, including back-ache, sciatica, lumbago, fibrositis, rheumatic pain and pain due to bruises, sprains, strains, stiff muscles and unbroken chilblains

Adult directions only given

Price: 100 ml £2.85, 200 ml £4.39

continued overleaf

Lloyd's Cream GSL

Cream containing diethylamine salicylate 10% w/w

Symptomatic relief of rheumatic pain, pain in fibrositis, soft-tissue rheumatism, lumbago, sciatica, inflammatory pains in muscles, ligaments, joints and sprains caused by injury or over-use, and stiffness after exercise

Children: not to be used in those under 6 years except on medical advice

Price: 30 g £3.45, 100 g £3.89

Movelat Relief Cream P

Cream containing salicylic acid 2% w/w, mucopolysaccharide polysulphate 0.2% w/w

Symptomatic relief of muscular pain and stiffness, sprains and strains, and pain due to rheumatic conditions

Children: not to be used

Price: 40 g £4.40, 80 g £6.99 A gel is also available 40 g £4.40, 80 g £6.99

PR Heat Spray GSL

Aerosol spray containing camphor 0.62% w/w, methyl salicylate 1.25% w/w, ethyl nicotinate 1.1% w/w

For relief of muscular and rheumatic pain, sprains, bruises and minor injuries where the skin is unbroken

Children: not to be used in those under 5 years

Price: 150 ml £3.35

Radian B Heat Spray GSL

Spray containing camphor 0.6% w/v, menthol 1.4% w/v, methyl salicylate 0.6% w/v, aspirin 1.2% w/v

Symptomatic relief of muscular and rheumatic aches and pains, including fibrositis, sciatica, lumbago, sprained ligaments, bruises, muscle stiffness, strains, tennis elbow and golf shoulder

Children: not recommended for those under 6 years

Price: 100 ml £2.49

Radian B Muscle Lotion GSL

Liniment containing camphor 0.6% w/v, menthol 1.4% w/v, salicylic acid 0.54% w/v, ammonium salicylate 1% w/v

continued opposite

Symptomatic relief of rheumatic and muscular pain, including general aches, aching neck, shoulders and back, pulled, sprained and stiff muscles, tennis elbow and golf shoulder. Also suitable for sports injuries

Children: not to be used for those under 6 years

Price: 125 ml £3.09, 500 ml £7.79

Radian B Muscle Rub GSL
Cream containing camphor 1.43% w/v, menthol 2.54% w/v, methyl salicylate 0.42% w/v, oleoresin capsicum 0.005% w/w

Symptomatic relief of muscular and rheumatic aches and pains, including general aches, aching neck, shoulders and back, and pulled, sprained and stiff muscles. Also suitable for sports injuries

Children: not recommended for those under 6 years

Price: 40 g £2.05, 100 g £3.69, 650 g £19.49

Ralgex Cream GSL
Cream containing glycol monosalicylate 10% w/w, methyl nicotinate 1% w/w, capsicum oleoresin 0.12% w/w

Symptomatic relief of muscular pain and stiffness, including backache, sciatica, sprains, lumbago, fibrositis and rheumatic pain

Children: not recommended except on medical advice

Price: 40 g £1.99, 100 g £3.75

Ralgex Freeze Spray GSL
Aerosol spray containing isopentane 67.77% w/w, methoxymethane 14.41% w/w, glycol monosalicylate 10% w/w

Symptomatic relief of muscular and rheumatic pain and sprains and stiffness, including backache, sciatica and lumbago

Children: not to be used for those under 5 years

Price: 125 ml £3.05

Ralgex Heat Spray GSL
Aerosol spray containing glycol monosalicylate 6% w/v, methyl nicotinate 1.6% w/v

Symptomatic relief of muscular and rheumatic pain and stiffness, sprains, backache, sciatica and lumbago

continued overleaf

Ralgex Heat Spray GSL *(cont.)*
Children: not to be used for those under 5 years

Price: 125 ml £3.05

Ralgex Stick GSL
Embrocation stick containing menthol 6.19% w/w, methyl salicylate 0.6% w/w, glycol salicylate 3.01% w/w, ethyl salicylate 3.01% w/w, capsicum oleoresin 1.96% w/w

Symptomatic relief of muscular and rheumatic pain, sprains and stiffness, including backache, sciatica and lumbago

Children: not recommended except on medical advice

Price: 32 g £2.49

Tiger Balm Red (extra strength) GSL
Ointment containing camphor 11% w/w, menthol 10% w/w, cajuput oil 7% w/w, clove oil 5% w/w

Temporary relief of minor or muscular aches and pains

Children: not to be used for those under 2 years

Price: red 19 g £4.39, white 19 g £4.19

Transvasin Heat Rub GSL
Cream containing ethyl nicotinate 2% w/w, hexyl nicotinate 2% w/w, tetrahydrofurfuryl salicylate 14% w/w

Relief of rheumatic and muscular aches and pains and the symptoms of sprains and strains

Adult directions only given

Price: 40 g £1.55, 80 g £2.65

Transvasin Heat Spray GSL
Spray containing 2-hydroxyethyl salicylate 5% w/w, diethylamine salicylate 5% w/w, methyl nicotinate 1% w/w

Symptomatic relief of muscular and rheumatic pain

Children: not to be used for those under 5 years

Price: 125 ml £2.69

Eye

Anti-infective eye preparations

Antibacterials

Propamidine isethionate

Brolene eye drops P

Eye drops containing propamidine isethionate 0.1% w/w

Treatment of minor eye infections such as conjunctivitis and blepharitis

Price: 10 ml £4.09

Brolene eye ointment P

Ointment containing dibromopropamidine isethionate 0.15% w/w

Treatment of minor eye and eyelid infections such as conjunctivitis and blepharitis

Price: 5 g £4.29

Anti-inflammatory preparations

Sodium cromoglicate

Clariteyes P
Solution containing sodium cromoglicate 2% w/v
Treatment of acute seasonal conjunctivitis, including hay fever
Price: 10 ml £4.45

Hay-Crom hay fever eye drops P
Solution containing sodium cromoglicate 2% w/v
Prophylaxis and treatment of seasonal allergic conjunctivitis
Price: 10 ml £3.99

Opticrom Allergy eye drops P
Solution containing sodium cromoglicate 2% w/v
For the relief and treatment of seasonal and perennial allergic conjunctivitis
Price: 5 ml £3.57, 10 ml £4.99

Optrex Allergy eye drops P
Eye drops containing sodium cromoglicate 2% w/v
Relief and treatment of seasonal allergic conjunctivitis
Price: 10 ml £4.59

Miscellaneous ophthalmic preparations

Tear deficiency, ocular lubricants and astringents

Carbomers

Gel Tears P

Eye drops containing carbomer 940 0.2% gel

Relief of dry eye conditions

Price: 5 g £2.89

Viscotears P

Liquid gel containing polyacrylic acid 0.2%

Treatment of tear deficiencies

Price: 10 g £4.62

Hydroxyethylcellulose

Minims Artificial Tears P

Preservative-free eye drops containing hydroxyethylcellulose 0.44%, sodium chloride 0.35%

Treatment of tear deficiencies

Price: 20 single-dose units £10.13

Hypromellose

Hypromellose eye drops (non-proprietary) P
Eye drops containing hypromellose 0.3%

Treatment of tear deficiency

Price varies

Isopto Alkaline P
Eye drops containing hypromellose 1%

Ocular lubricant

Price: 10 ml £1.75

Isopto Plain P
Eye drops containing hypromellose 0.5%

Emollient, treatment of tear deficiencies

Price: 10 ml £1.50

Tears Naturale P
Eye drops containing dextran 70 0.1%, hypromellose 0.3%

Treatment of tear deficiencies

Price: 15 ml £2.96

Hypromellose with phenylephrine

Isopto Frin P
Eye drops containing phenylephrine hydrochloride 0.12%, hypro-mellose 0.5%

Temporary relief of eye redness due to minor irritations

Price: 10 ml £2.01

Hamamelis

Optrex eye drops P
Eye drops containing witch hazel, distilled 13% v/v

Relief of minor eye irritations caused by dusty or smoky atmospheres, driving or close work

Children: not recommended for those under 3 years except on medical advice

Price: 10 ml £3.25, 18 ml £3.99

Optrex eye lotion GSL
Solution containing witch hazel distilled 13% v/v

Relief of minor eye irritations caused by dusty or smoky atmospheres, driving or close work

Children: not recommended for those under 3 years except on medical advice

Price: 110 ml £2.99, 110 ml + bath £3.45, 300 ml + bath £4.59

Hamamelis with naphazoline

Optrex Clear Eyes eye drops P
Eye drops containing naphazoline hydrochloride 0.01% w/v, witch hazel distilled 12.5% v/v

Temporary relief of redness of the eye due to minor eye irritations

Children: not recommended

Price: 10 ml £3.45

Liquid paraffin

Lacri-Lube P
Preservative-free ointment containing lanolin alcohols 0.2% w/w, mineral oil 42.5% w/w, white petroleum jelly 57.3% w/w

To lubricate and protect dry eyes, particularly at night

Price: 3.5 g £3.35, 5 g £4.35

Lubri-Tears P
Preservative-free ointment containing white soft paraffin 60%, liquid paraffin 30%, wool fat 10%

Ocular lubricant, used for corneal protection

Price: 5 g £4.03

Paraffin, yellow soft

Simple Eye Ointment (non-proprietary) P
Ointment containing in yellow soft paraffin liquid paraffin 10%, wool fat 10%

To lubricate the eye surface

Price varies

Polyvinyl alcohol

Hypotears P

Eye drops containing polyvinyl alcohol 1%

Treatment of tear deficiencies

Price: 15 ml £1.92

Liquifilm Tears P

Solution containing liquifilm 1.4% w/v

Lubricant for the relief of dry eye symptoms

Price: 15 ml £2.84 A preservative-free version is also available: 30 single-use units £8.25

Refresh Ophthalmic Solution P

Solution containing liquifilm 1.4% w/v

Refreshes the eyes and treats the symptoms associated with dry eye, typically tired eyes, soreness, burning or itching

Price: 30 single-use vials £4.29

Sno Tears P

Eye drops containing polyvinyl alcohol 1.4%

Ocular lubricant

Price: 10 ml £1.94

Povidone

Oculotect P

Eye drops containing povidone 5%

Relief of dry eyes

Price: 20 single-dose units £5.70

Sodium chloride

Minims Sodium Chloride P
Preservative-free eye drops containing sodium chloride 0.9%

For irrigation of the eye

Price: 20 single-dose units £8.67

Ear, nose and oropharynx

Drugs that act on the ear

Anti-infective preparations

Earcalm Spray P
60 mg metered-dose ear spray containing acetic acid (glacial) Ph Eur 2% w/w

Treatment of superficial infections of the external auditory canal

Price: 5 ml £6.38

Analgesic preparations

Choline salicylate

Audax ear drops P
Solution containing choline salicylate solution 20% w/v, glycerine 12.6% w/v

Symptomatic relief of ear pain in acute and chronic otitis media and externa. For the softening of ear wax, to aid ear wax removal

Children: not to be used for those under 1 year except on medical advice

Price: 10 ml £3.99

Earex Plus ear drops P
Ear drops containing choline salicylate solution 43.22% w/v, glycerine 12.62% w/v

Symptomatic relief of ear pain in acute and chronic otitis media. For the softening of ear wax, to aid ear wax removal

Children: not to be used for those under 1 year without medical advice

Price: 10 ml £3.99

Removal of ear wax

Cerumol ear drops P

Liquid containing arachis oil 57.3% w/v, chlorobutanol 5% w/v, *p*-dichlorobenzene 1949 2% w/v

To loosen wax in the external ear canal

Adult directions only given

Price: 11 ml £2.55

Earex ear drops GSL

Oily liquid containing almond oil 33.33% v/v, arachis oil 33.33% v/v, camphor oil rectified 33.33% v/v

For easy removal of ear wax

Price: 10 ml £2.59

Exterol ear drops P

Viscous ear drops containing urea hydrogen peroxide 5% w/w

To aid the removal of hardened ear wax

Price: 8 ml £3.09

Molcer ear drops P

Ear drops containing in 1 ml dioctyl sodium sulphosuccinate 5% w/w

For the softening of ear wax prior to its removal by syringing with warm water

Price: 15 ml £2.33

Otex ear drops P

Viscous solution containing urea hydrogen peroxide 5% w/w

To aid removal of hardened wax, thus reducing the need to syringe

Price: 8 ml £4.25

Wax Wane ear drops GSL

Ear drops containing turpentine oil 15% v/v, chloroxylenol 0.2% w/v, terpineol 5% v/v

To soften hard wax in the ear before its removal by gentle syringing

Price: 10 ml £1.72

Drugs that act on the nose

Drugs used in nasal allergy

Antihistamines

Levocabastine

Livostin Direct nasal spray P
Microsuspension containing in 1 ml levocabastine hydrochloride 0.54 mg
Symptomatic treatment of seasonal allergic rhinitis
Children: dosage given for 12 years and over
Price: 5 ml £5.75

Corticosteroids

Beclometasone dipropionate

Beconase Allergy P
Aqueous nasal metered-dose spray containing per dose beclometasone dipropionate 50 µg
Prevention and treatment of common symptoms of allergic rhinitis, including hay fever and all other airborne allergies, such as sneezing or blocked nose and runny or itchy nose and eyes
Children: not recommended for those under 18 years of age
Price: 110 sprays £5.99, 180 sprays £8.99

Nasobec Hayfever P
Nasal spray containing beclometasone dipropionate 50 µg
To treat and prevent the symptoms of allergic reactions to pollens, house dust and animal fur, such as itchy or runny nose and sneezing
Children: not recommended
Price: spray £6.99

Sodium cromoglicate

Rynacrom Allergy nasal spray P
Metered-dose aqueous aerosol containing sodium cromoglicate 2% w/v

Xylometazoline hydrochloride 0.025% w/v

For the prophylaxis and treatment of allergic rhinitis (seasonal and perennial) where this is accompanied by nasal congestion

Price: 10 ml £5.29

Topical nasal decongestants

Oxymetazoline hydrochloride

Afrazine nasal spray GSL
Nasal spray containing oxymetazoline hydrochloride 0.05% w/v

Relief of nasal congestion associated with a wide variety of allergic and infectious upper respiratory tract disorders

Children: not recommended for those under 5 years

Price: 15 ml £2.69

Dristan nasal spray GSL
Nasal spray containing oxymetazoline hydrochloride 0.05% w/w

Relief of the symptoms of acute rhinitis in head colds, hay fever, catarrh and nasal congestion

Children: not recommended for those under 6 years

Price: 15 ml £2.99

Vicks Sinex Decongestant nasal spray GSL
Non-pressurised aqueous nasal spray solution containing oxy-metazoline hydrochloride 0.05% w/v

Symptomatic relief of congestion of the upper respiratory tract due to the common cold, hay fever or sinusitis

Children: not to be used in those under 6 years

Price: 20 ml £3.49

Phenylephrine hydrochloride

Fenox nasal drops P

Viscous liquid containing phenylephrine hydrochloride 0.5% w/v

Relief of nasal congestion due to head colds, catarrh, sinusitis and hay fever

Children: not recommended for those under 5 years except on medical advice

Price: 15 ml £2.99 Also available as spray 15 ml £2.99

Xylometazoline hydrochloride

Otradrops Adult GSL
Solution containing xylometazoline hydrochloride 0.1% w/v

Symptomatic relief of nasal congestion, perennial and allergic rhinitis and sinusitis

Children: dosage given for 12 years of age and over

Price: 10 ml £2.39 Also available as spray 10 ml £2.59

Otradrops Paediatric GSL
Solution containing xylometazoline hydrochloride 0.05% w/v

Symptomatic relief of nasal congestion, perennial and allergic rhinitis and sinusitis

Children: dosages given for 2–12 years of age

Price: 10 ml £2.29

Otrivine Adult Formula nasal drops GSL
Nasal drops containing xylometazoline hydrochloride 0.1% w/v

Symptomatic relief of nasal congestion, perennial and allergic rhinitis and sinusitis

Children: should not be used

Price: 10 ml £2.59 Also available as spray 10 ml £2.75, menthol spray 10 ml £2.79 and measured-dose spray 10 ml £3.59

Otrivine Children's Formula nasal drops GSL
Nasal drops containing xylometazoline hydrochloride 0.05% w/v

Symptomatic relief of nasal congestion, perennial and allergic rhinitis and sinusitis

Children: not to be used for infants under 3 months

Price: 10 ml £2.39

Sudafed Decongestant nasal spray GSL
Aqueous metered-dose nasal spray containing xylometazoline hydrochloride 0.1% w/v

Symptomatic relief of nasal congestion associated with the common cold, influenza, sinusitis, allergic and non-allergic rhinitis and other upper respiratory tract allergies

Children: should not be used

Price: 15 ml £3.45

continued opposite

Tixycolds Cold and Allergy nasal drops GSL
Nasal drops containing xylometazoline hydrochloride 0.05% w/v

Treatment of nasal congestion, perennial and allergic rhinitis and sinusitis

Children: not recommended for those under 2 years except on medical advice

Price: 10 ml £2.39

Drugs that act on the oropharynx

Drugs used for oral ulceration and inflammation

Benzydamine hydrochloride

Difflam oral rinse P
Liquid containing benzydamine hydrochloride 0.15%

Painful inflammatory conditions of the mouth and throat

Children: oral rinse not recommended

Price: 300 ml £7.23 Spray also available 30 ml £5.99

Carbenoxolone

Bioral gel P
Gel containing carbenoxolone sodium 2% w/w

Treatment of mouth ulcers

Price: 5 g £3.85

Carmellose sodium

Orabase GSL
Paste containing carmellose sodium 16.7%, pectin 16.7%, gelatin 16.7% in Plastibase
Protects lesions of oral mucosa and moist body surfaces
Price: 30 g £3.19, 100 g £7.10

Orahesive GSL
Powder containing carmellose sodium, pectin and gelatin in equal parts
Protects lesions of oral mucosa and moist body surfaces
Price: 25 g £3.68

Cetrimide

Bansor mouth antiseptic GSL
Viscous solution containing cetrimide 0.01% w/v
Relief of symptoms of sore gums in children and adults
Price: 25 ml 97p

Corticosteroids

Adcortyl in Orabase for Mouth Ulcers P
Paste containing triamcinolone acetonide 0.1% w/w
Treatment of mouth ulcers
Price: 5 g £3.95

Local anaesthetics

Anbesol Adult Strength Gel P
Gel containing lidocaine hydrochloride 2% w/w, cetylpyridium chloride 0.02% w/w, chlorocresol 0.1% w/w
Temporary relief of pain caused by recurrent mouth ulcers and denture irritation
Children: not recommended
Price: 10 g £2.25

Anbesol Liquid P
Liquid containing lidocaine hydrochloride 0.9% w/w, cetylpyridium chloride 0.02% w/w, chlorocresol 0.1% w/w
Temporary relief of pain caused by recurrent mouth ulcers, denture irritation and teething
Price: 6.5 ml £2.19, 15 ml £4.05

Anbesol Teething Gel P
Gel containing lidocaine hydrochloride 1% w/w, cetylpyridium chloride 0.02% w/w, chlorocresol 0.1% w/w
Temporary relief of pain caused by recurrent mouth ulcers, denture irritation and teething
Price: 10 g £1.99

Calgel Teething Gel GSL
Sugar-free gel containing cetylpyridium chloride 0.1% w/w
Relieves teething pain and soothes infants' gums. Also has mild antiseptic properties
Children: directions given for those aged 3 months and over
Price: 10 g £1.99

Dentinox Teething Gel GSL
Gel containing lidocaine hydrochloride 0.33% w/w, cetylpyridium chloride 0.1% w/w
Relieves teething pains and soothes gums
Price: 15 g £2.25

Medijel Gel GSL
Gel containing lidocaine hydrochloride 0.66% w/w, aminacrine hydrochloride 0.05% w/w

continued overleaf

Medijel Gel GSL *(cont.)*
Relief from pain of common mouth ulcers, sore gums and denture rubbing
Price: 15 g £2.55

Medijel Pastilles P
Soft pastille containing lidocaine hydrochloride 0.25% w/w, aminacrine hydrochloride 0.025% w/w
Relief from pain of common mouth ulcers, sore gums and denture rubbing
Price: 25 £2.55

Rinstead Adult Gel P
Sugar-free gel containing benzocaine 2% w/w, chloroxylenol 0.106% w/w
Symptomatic relief of pain due to mouth ulcers, sore areas caused by denture rubbing, and soreness of the mouth
Children: not recommended
Price: 15 g £3.09

Rinstead Contact Pastilles P
Sugar-free pastille containing lidocaine hydrochloride 2 mg
For rapid relief from pain due to mouth ulcers, sore gums and denture rubbing
Children: directions given for those aged 5 years and over
Price: 6 £2.59

Rinstead Teething Gel GSL
Sugar-free gel containing lidocaine 0.5% w/w, cetylpyridium chloride 0.1% w/w
Temporary relief of pain caused by mouth ulcers and teething
Price: 15 g £2.35

Woodward's Teething Gel GSL
Gel containing lidocaine hydrochloride 0.5% w/w, cetylpyridium chloride 0.025% w/w
Relief of pain associated with teething problems
Children: not recommended for babies under 3 months
Price: 10 g £2.15

Menthol

Rinstead Sugar-Free Pastilles GSL
Pastille containing cetylpyridium chloride 0.128% w/w, menthol 0.033% w/w

Temporary relief of pain and discomfort associated with recurrent mouth ulcers and sore spots caused by denture rubbing

Children: not recommended

Price: 24 £2.55

Choline salicylate

Bonjela Oral Pain-Relieving Gel GSL
Gel containing cetalkonium chloride 0.01% w/w, choline salicylate 8.714% w/w

Relief of pain and discomfort associated with common mouth ulcers, cold sores, sore spots caused by denture rubbing, and infant teething

Children: not recommended for infants under 4 months

Price: 15 g £2.55

Dinneford's Teejel Gel GSL
Gel containing choline salicylate 8.7% w/w, cetalkonium chloride 0.01% w/w

Relief of pain and discomfort in mouth ulcers arising from minor recurrent aphthous ulceration, and in cold sores, infant teething and denture irritation

Children: not to be used in infants under 4 months of age

Price: 10 g £2.29

Salicylic acid

Pyralvex P

Liquid containing extract of anthraquinone glycosides 5%, salicylic acid 1%

Relief of pain and discomfort due to mouth ulcers or denture irritation

Children: not recommended

Price: 10 ml £2.49

Oropharyngeal anti-infective drugs

Fungal infections

Miconazole

Daktarin Oral Gel P

Gel containing miconazole base 2% w/w

Treatment of fungal infestation of the oropharynx

Price: 15 g £3.99

Lozenges and sprays

Beechams Throat-Plus Lemon Lozenges GSL
Lozenge containing hexylresorcinol 2.5 mg, benzalkonium chloride solution 1.2 mg
Symptomatic relief of sore throat and associated pain
Children: not to be given to those under 7 years
Price: 24 £2.05 Also available in blackcurrant flavour

Bradosol Sugar Free Original Citrus Lozenges GSL
Lozenge containing benzalkonium chloride 0.5 mg
Symptomatic relief of sore throat
Children: not recommended for those under 5 years
Price: 20 £1.95 Also available in cherry menthol flavour

Dequadin Lozenges P
Lozenge containing dequalinium chloride 0.25 mg
Treatment of common infections of the mouth and throat
Children: not to be given to those under 10 years
Price: 20 £1.95, 40 £3.29

Labosept Pastilles GSL
Sugar-free pastille containing dequalinium chloride 0.25 mg
Treatment of sore throat
Price: 20 £1.54

Lemsip Sore Throat Antibacterial GSL
Lozenge containing hexylresorcinol 2.4 mg
Antiseptic, demulcent and local anaesthetic relief of sore throat and associated pain
Children: not recommended for those under 6 years
Price: 24 £2.05

Mentholatum Antiseptic Lozenges GSL
Lozenge containing eucalyptus oil 8.57 mg, menthol 11.43 mg, amylmetacresol 0.43 mg

continued overleaf

Mentholatum Antiseptic Lozenges GSL *(cont.)*
Symptomatic relief of coughs, head colds, nasal congestion and sore throat
Children: not recommended for those under 3 years
Price: 12 75p

Merocets Lozenges GSL
Lozenge containing cetylpyridinium chloride 1.4 mg
Symptomatic relief of sore throat and other symptoms associated with mouth and throat infections
Children: not recommended for those under 6 years
Price: 24 £2.09

Merocets Plus GSL
Lozenge containing menthol 5 mg, cetylpyridinium chloride 1.4 mg, eucalyptus oil 3 mg
Symptomatic relief of sore throat, nasal congestion, and minor irritations of the mouth and throat
Children: not recommended for those under 6 years
Price: 24 £2.09

Strepsils Extra GSL
Lozenge containing hexylresorcinol 2.4 mg
Relief of sore throat and associated pain
Children: not to be given to those under 6 years
Price: 24 £2.29

Strepsils Original GSL
Lozenge containing amylmetacresol 0.6 mg, dichlorobenzyl (2,4-)alcohol 1.2 mg
Symptomatic relief of mouth and throat infections, including sore throats
Price: 24 £2.10 Also available in honey and lemon, and menthol and eucalyptus flavours. Sugar-free version is also available: 16 £2.05

Strepsils with Vitamin C GSL
Lozenge containing vitamin C 100 mg, amylmetacresol 0.6 mg, dichlorobenzyl (2,4-)alcohol 1.2 mg

continued opposite

Symptomatic relief of mouth and throat infections, including sore throat

Price: 24 £2.10

TCP Sore Throat Lozenges GSL
Lozenge containing hexylresorcinol 2.4 mg

Relief of sore throat and associated pain

Children: not to be given to those under 6 years

Price: 24 £1.95

Lozenges and sprays containing local anaesthetics

AAA Mouth and Throat Spray P

Aerosol spray containing in each metered dose benzocaine 1.5 mg

Relief of pain associated with sore throat and minor mouth infections

Children: not recommended for those under 6 years

Price: 60 doses £4.15

Bradosol Plus (sugar-free) P

Lozenge containing lidocaine hydrochloride 5 mg, domiphen bromide 0.5 mg

Symptomatic relief of sore throat

Children: not recommended

Price: 20 £2.35

Dequacaine Lozenges P

Lozenge containing benzocaine 10 mg, dequalinium chloride 0.25 mg

For severe sore throats

Children: not recommended

Price: 24 £2.75

Merocaine Lozenges P

Lozenge containing benzocaine 10 mg, cetylpyridinium chloride 1.4 mg

Temporary relief of pain and discomfort in sore throat and superficial minor mouth infections

Children: should not be given

Price: 24 £2.55

Strepsils Pain Relief Plus P

Lozenge containing lidocaine hydrochloride 10 mg, amylmetacresol 0.6 mg, dichlorobenzyl (2,4-)alcohol 1.2 mg

Symptomatic relief of mouth and throat infections, including severe sore throats

Children: not recommended

Price: 24 £2.55

continued opposite

Strepsil Pain Relief Spray P
Spray containing lidocaine hydrochloride 2% w/v

Symptomatic relief of sore throats

Children: not recommended

Price: 20 ml £4.39

Tyrozets P
Lozenge containing benzocaine 5 mg, tyothricin 1 mg

Relief of sore throats and minor mouth irritations

Children: not recommended for those under 3 years

Price: 24 £2.25

Vicks Ultra Chloraseptic P
Throat spray containing benzocaine 0.71% w/v

Symptomatic relief of sore throat pain

Children: not to be used for those under 6 years

Price: 15 ml £4.49

Mouthwashes, gargles and dentrifices

Chlorhexidine gluconate

Corsodyl Dental Gel P
Gel containing chlorhexidine gluconate 1% w/w

Inhibits formation of dental plaque. Aids treatment and prevention of gingivitis and maintenance of oral hygiene. Useful in the management of recurrent aphthous ulceration and recurrent candidal infection

Price: 50 g £2.65

Corsodyl Original Mouthwash P
Solution containing chlorhexidine gluconate 0.2% w/v

Aids treatment and prevention of gingivitis, maintenance of oral hygiene and inhibition of dental plaque. Also used in post-periodontal surgery regimes to promote gingival healing. Useful in aphthous ulceration and oral candidal infection

Price: 300 ml £4.15 Also available in mint flavour, and as a spray 60 ml £6.69

Hexetidine

Oraldene GSL
Solution containing hexetidine 0.1% w/v

Treatment of minor mouth infections, including thrush, and as an aid to the prevention and treatment of gingivitis, and in the management of sore throat and recurrent aphthous ulcers. It is also valuable in halitosis and before and after dental surgery

Children: not to be used for those under 6 years

Price: 100 ml £2.19, 200 ml £3.39

Oxidising agents

Bocasan P
Mouthwash granules containing sodium perborate monohydrate 68.6%, sodium hydrogen tartrate (anhydrous) 29.4%

Treatment of gingivitis and stomatitis

Price: 20 £2.65

Povidone–iodine

Betadine Gargle and Mouthwash P
Solution containing povidone–iodine 1% w/v

Treatment of viral, fungal and bacterial mouth and throat infections, and for oral hygiene prior to, during and after dental and oral surgery

Children: not recommended for those under 6 years

Price: 250 ml £1.95

Thymol

Compound Thymol Glycerin BP 1988 (non-proprietary) GSL
Solution containing glycerol 10%, thymol 0.05%

Used to maintain oral hygiene

Price varies

Treatment of dry mouth

Luborant P
Solution containing carboxymethylcellulose 390 mg

Treatment of dry mouth

Children: not recommended

Price: 60 ml spray £6.98

Skin

Emollients and bath preparations

Emollients

Aqueous Cream BP (non-proprietary) GSL
Emulsifying ointment 30%, phenoxyethanol 1%

For dry skin conditions

Price varies

Emulsifying Ointment BP (non-proprietary) GSL
Emulsifying wax 30%, white soft paraffin 50%, liquid paraffin 20%

For dry skin conditions

Price varies

Paraffin, White Soft BP (non-proprietary) GSL
White petroleum jelly

For dry skin conditions

Price varies

Paraffin, Yellow Soft BP (non-proprietary) GSL
Yellow petroleum jelly

For dry skin conditions

Price varies

E45 Cream GSL
Cream containing white soft paraffin BP 14.5% w/w, light liquid paraffin 12.6% w/w, hypoallergenic anhydrous lanolin 1% w/w

Symptomatic relief of dry skin conditions where the use of an emollient is indicated, such as flaking, chapped skin, ichthyosis, traumatic dermatitis, sunburn, the dry stage of eczema, and certain dry cases of psoriasis

Price: 50 g £1.85, 125 g £3.75, 500 g £8.79

E45 Lotion GSL
Cream containing white soft paraffin 10% w/w, light liquid paraffin 4% w/w, hypoallergenic anhydrous lanolin 1% w/w

continued opposite

Symptomatic relief of dry skin conditions such as those associated with atopic eczema and contact dermatitis

Price: 200 ml £3.39, 500 ml £6.39

E45 Emollient Wash Cream GSL
Cleanser containing zinc oxide 5% w/w, mineral oils 79.5% w/w

A cleansing emollient for the symptomatic relief of endogenous and exogenous eczema, xeroderma, ichthyosis and senile pruritis associated with dry skin

Price: 250 ml £4.49

Epaderm GSL
Emulsifying ointment containing emulsifying wax 30% w/w, yellow soft paraffin 30% w/w

For general use as an emollient to moisturise and soften dry skin. May be used instead of soap

Price: 125 g £6.45, 500 g £10.95

Hydromol Cream GSL
Cream containing liquid paraffin 10% w/w, sodium pyrrolidine carboxylate 2.5% w/w, arachis oil 10% w/w, isopropyl myristate 5% w/w, sodium lactate 1% w/w

An emollient cream to lubricate and hydrate dry skin

Price: 50 g £3.60, 100 g £6.70, 500 g £22.21

Morhulin Ointment GSL
Ointment containing zinc oxide 38% w/w, cod liver oil 11.4% w/w

Treatment of minor wounds, minor excoriations, pressure sores, varicose ulcers, eczema and napkin rash

Price: 50 g £2.19, 350 g £8.99

Oilatum Cream GSL
Cream containing arachis oil 21% w/w

Management of dry, sensitive skin, lanolin sensitivity and alkali intolerance

Price: 40 g £3.16, 80 g £4.90

Oilatum Hand Aquagel GSL
Emollient gel containing liquid paraffin light 70% w/w

continued overleaf

Oilatum Hand Aquagel GSL (*cont.*)
Treatment of dry skin conditions

Price: 50 g £4.35

Unguentum M GSL
Cream containing colloidal anhydrous silica (0.1%), liquid paraffin (3%), white soft paraffin (32%), cetostearyl alcohol (9%), polysorbate (40.6%), glycerol monostearate (3%), MCT (2%), sorbic acid (0.2%), propylene glycol (5%)

Symptomatic treatment of dermatitis, nappy rash, ichthyosis and eczema, protection of raw and abraded skin areas, pruritis and related conditions where dry scaly skin is a problem. Also used as a pre-bathing emollient for dry/eczematous skin

Price: 60 g £5.25

Emollients containing urea

E45 Itch Relief Cream GSL
Cream containing lauromacrogols 3% w/w, urea 5% w/w

Treats and soothes itching caused by eczema, dermatitis, pruritis and other dry skin conditions

Price: 50 g £3.29

Emollient bath additives

Balneum GSL
Liquid containing soya oil 84.75% w/w

Dry skin indications including those associated with dermatitis and eczema

Price: 150 ml £5.45

Balneum Plus GSL
Liquid containing soya oil 82.95% w/w, lauromacrogols 15% w/w

Treatment of dry skin disorders such as eczema and dermatitis where itching is a problem

Price: 150 ml £5.99

Dermol 200 Shower Emollient P
Emollient containing benzalkonium chloride 0.1% w/w, chlorhexidine hydrochloride 0.1% w/w, isopropyl myristate 2.5% w/w, liquid paraffin 2.5% w/w

For the management of dry and pruritic skin conditions, especially eczema and dermatitis

Price: 200 ml £7.04

E45 Emollient Bath Oil GSL
Oil containing mineral oil 91% w/w, dimeticone cetyl 5% w/w

Symptomatic relief of endogenous and exogenous eczema, xeroderma, ichthyosis and senile pruritis associated with dry skin

Price: 250 ml £4.49, 500 ml £7.15

Emulsiderm Emollient P
Liquid emulsion containing benzalkonium chloride 0.5% w/w, isopropyl myristate 25% w/w, liquid paraffin 25% w/w

For the treatment of dry skin conditions, including eczema and psoriasis

Price: 300 ml £7.64, 1 litre £23.78

Hydromol Emollient GSL
Liquid containing liquid paraffin 37.8% v/v, liquid paraffin light 37.8%, isopropyl myristate 13% v/v

A semi-dispersible bath additive for the treatment of dry skin conditions such as eczema, ichthyosis and senile pruritis

Price: 150 ml £3.30, 350 ml £6.70, 1 litre £15.86

continued overleaf

Oilatum Bath Formula GSL
Liquid containing liquid paraffin light 63.4% w/w

Treatment of contact dermatitis, eczema, senile pruritis, ichthyosis and related dry skin conditions

Price: 150 ml £4.79, 300 ml £8.65 Oilatum Junior is also available

Oilatum Junior Flare-Up GSL
Liquid containing benzalkonium chloride solution 6% w/w, liquid paraffin light 52.5% w/w, triclosan 2% w/w

Topical treatment of eczema flare-up

Price: 150 ml £6.25

Barrier preparations

Zinc Ointment (non-proprietary) GSL
Ointment containing in Simple Ointment BP zinc oxide 15%

Treatment of nappy and urinary rash and eczematous conditions

Price varies

Zinc and Castor Oil Ointment BP (non-proprietary) GSL
Ointment containing zinc oxide 15%, castor oil 50%, arachis oil 30.5%, white beeswax 10%, cetostearyl alcohol 2%

Treatment of nappy and urinary rash

Price varies

Metanium Ointment GSL
Ointment containing titanium dioxide 20% w/w, titanium peroxide 5% w/w, titanium salicylate 3% w/w

Treatment of nappy rash

Price: 30 g £2.99

Sudocrem Antiseptic Healing Cream GSL
Cream containing zinc oxide 15.25% w/w, benzyl alcohol 0.39% w/w, lanolin anhydrous hypoallergenic 4% w/w, benzyl benzoate 1.01% w/w, benzyl cinnamate 0.15% w/w

Treatment of nappy rash, incontinence dermatitis, bedsores, surface wounds, minor burns, eczema, chilblains, acne and sunburn

Price: 60 g £1.59, 125 g £2.49, 250 g £4.29, 400 g £6.29

Vasogen Cream GSL
Cream containing zinc oxide 7.5% w/w, calamine 1.5% w/w, dimeticone 20% w/w

Prevention and treatment of nappy rash and bedsores, and local protection of the skin around the stoma after ileostomy and colostomy

Price: 50 g £1.23, 100 g £2.09

Topical local anaesthetics and antipruritics

Topical antipruritics

Calamine

Calamine Aqueous Cream (non-proprietary) GSL
Cream containing calamine 4%, zinc oxide 3%, liquid paraffin 20%, glycerol monostearate 5%, cetomacrogol emulsifying wax 5%, phenoxyethanol 0.5%

Treatment of pruritis

Price varies

Calamine Lotion (non-proprietary) GSL
Lotion containing calamine 15%, zinc oxide 5%, glycerol 5%, bentonite 3%, sodium citrate 0.5%, liquefied phenol 0.5%

Treatment of pruritis

Price varies

Calamine Oily Lotion (non-proprietary) GSL
Lotion containing calamine 5%, arachis oil 50%, oleic acid 0.5%, wool fat 1% in calcium hydroxide solution

Treatment of pruritis

Price varies

Crotamiton

Eurax Cream GSL
Cream containing crotamiton 10% w/w

Relief of itching and skin irritation caused by sunburn, dry eczema, itchy dermatitis, allergic rashes, hives, nettle rash, chicken-pox, insect bites and stings, heat rashes and personal itching. Treatment of scabies

Children: not recommended for those under 3 years except on medical advice

Price: 30 g £3.49, 100 g £5.99 Lotion also available 100 ml £4.49

Topical local anaesthetics

Burneze spray P

Aerosol spray containing benzocaine 1% w/w

Symptomatic relief of pain from minor, superficial burns and scalds where the skin is unbroken

Price: 60 ml £4.89

Dermidex Cream P

Cream containing chlorbutanol 1% w/w, lidocaine base 1.2% w/w, cetrimide 0.5% w/w, aluminium chlorohydroallantoinate 0.25% w/w

Relief of mild pain caused by minor skin cuts, scratches and grazes (chapping) and soreness caused by detergents, soaps, deodorants, jewellery, and bites and stings

Children: not recommended for those under 4 years

Price: 30 g £3.35, 50 g £5.30

Lanacane Creme GSL

Cream emulsion containing benzocaine 3% w/w

Symptomatic relief of minor pain, itching and irritation in localised skin conditions, such as insect bites, nettle stings, minor skin abrasions and external genital and external anal itching

Children: should not be used

Price: 30 g £3.39, 60 g £5.65

Solarcaine Cream P

Cream containing benzocaine 1% w/w, triclosan 0.2% w/w

Relief of sunburn pain, minor burns, skin injuries and insect bites

Children: not to be used in those under 3 years

Price: 25 ml £3.19 Lotion also available 75 ml £4.09

Solarcaine Gel P

Gel containing lignocaine hydrochloride 0.5% w/w

Relief of sunburn pain, minor burns, skin injuries and insect bites

Children: directions given for age 3 years and over

Price: 135 g £4.69

Solarcaine Spray P

Aerosol liquid containing benzocaine 2.857% w/w, triclosan 0.057% w/w

continued overleaf

Solarcaine Spray P (*cont.*)
Relief of sunburn pain, minor burns, skin injuries and insect bites
Children: not to be used in those under 3 years
Price: 95 g £4.95

Vagisil Medicated Creme GSL
Cream containing lidocaine 2% w/w
Cools, soothes and relieves feminine itching, burning and irritation, and helps to prevent further irritation by reducing the urge to scratch
Children: not suitable
Price: 30 g £3.55

Topical antihistamines

Anthisan Cream P
Cream containing mepyramine maleate 2% w/w
Symptomatic relief of insect bites and stings and nettle-rash
Price: 25g £3.29

Caladryl Cream P
Cream containing camphor 0.1% w/w, zinc oxide 8% w/w, diphenhydramine hydrochloride 1% w/w
Relief of irritation associated with urticaria and other minor skin affections, and alleviation of the discomforts of sunburn, prickly heat, insect bites and nettle stings. Relief of hives in infants
Price: 42 g £3.55 Lotion also available 125 ml £3.55

Histergan Cream P
Cream containing diphenhydramine hydrochloride 2% w/w
Symptomatic relief of allergic itching, allergic rashes, stings and insect bites
Children: not to be used for those under 6 years of age
Price: 25 g £3.38

Wasp-Eze Ointment P
Cream containing antazoline hydrochloride 2% w/w
Short-term relief of wasp stings and other insect bites
Children: directions given for age 1 year and over
Price: 15 g £2.59

Topical local anaesthetics plus topical antihistamine

Anthisan Plus Sting Relief Spray P

Metered-dose spray containing benzocaine 2% w/w, mepyramine maleate 2% w/w

Symptomatic relief of insect bites and stings, and jellyfish and nettle stings

Children: directions given for age 3 years and over

Price: 60 doses £3.79

Wasp-Eze Spray P

Aerosol spray containing benzocaine 1% w/w, mepyramine maleate 0.5% w/w

Treatment of all insect bites and stings, nettle stings and jellyfish stings

Price: 30 ml £3.59, 60 ml £4.85

Topical corticosteroids

Hydrocortisone

Dermacort Cream P
Cream containing hydrocortisone 0.1% w/w

Treatment of irritant contact dermatitis, mild to moderate eczema, allergic contact dermatitis and rashes due to reactions to plants, insect bites, jewellery, toiletries, deodorants, soaps and detergents

Children: not recommended for those under 10 years except on medical advice

Price: 15 g £2.80

HC45 Hydrocortisone Cream P
Cream containing hydrocortisone acetate 1% w/w

Treatment of irritant contact dermatitis, allergic contact dermatitis, insect bite reactions and mild to moderate eczema

Children: not recommended for those under 10 years except on medical advice

Price: 15 g £3.15

Lanacort Cream P
Cream containing hydrocortisone acetate UF powder 1% w/w

Treatment of mild to moderate eczema, irritant dermatitis, contact allergic dermatitis and insect bite reactions

Children: not to be used for those under 10 years except on medical advice

Price: 15 g £2.95 Ointment also available

Hydrocortisone with crotamiton

Eurax HC cream P
Cream containing crotamiton 10% w/w, hydrocortisone 0.25% w/w

Relief of inflammation and pruritis associated with irritant and allergic contact dermatitis, insect bite reactions and mild to moderate eczema

Children: not recommended for use under 10 years of age

Price: 15 g £3.05

Hydrocortisone with antifungals

Canesten Hydrocortisone P
Cream containing clotrimazole 1% w/w, hydrocortisone 1% w/w
Treatment of inflamed candidal intertrigo
Price: 15 g £4.79

Preparations for psoriasis

Coal tar and dithranol preparations

Coal tar

Exorex Lotion GSL
Emulsion containing prepared coal tar 1973 1% w/w
Relief and treatment of psoriasis and eczema of the skin and scalp
Price: 100 ml £14.95, 250 ml £29.95

Gelcotar P
Gel containing coal tar solution strong 5% w/w, tar 5% w/w
Treatment of psoriasis and dermatitis in the chronic phase
Price: 50 g £5.39, 500 g £27.97

Coal tar with salicylic acid

Gelcosal P
Gel containing salicylic acid 2% w/w, coal tar solution strong 5% w/w, tar 5% w/w
Treatment of psoriasis or dermatitis in the chronic scaling phase
Price: 50 g £5.99

Dithranol

Dithrocream P

Cream containing dithranol 0.1% or 0.25%

Treatment of sub-acute and chronic psoriasis

Price: 0.1% 50 g £6.64, 0.25% 50 g £7.13 Dithrocream Forte 0.5% cream: 50 g £8.21 and Dithrocream HP 1% cream: 50 g £9.56

Micanol P

Cream containing dithranol 1%

Treatment of sub-acute and chronic psoriasis, including scalp psoriasis using short contact method

Price: 50 g £14.06

Dithranol with salicylic acid

Psorin Scalp Gel P

Gel containing dithranol 0.25%, salicylic acid 1.6%

Treatment of scalp psoriasis

Price: 50 g £6.99

Dithranol with coal tar and salicylic acid

Psorin P

Ointment containing coal tar 1%, dithranol 0.11%, salicylic acid 1.6%

Treatment of sub-acute and chronic (stable) psoriasis

Price: 50 g £8.48

Herbal preparations

Potter's Psorasolv Ointment GSL
Ointment containing sulphur 7% w/w, zinc oxide 7% w/w, starch 5% w/w, poke root liquid extract 0.5% w/w, clivers soft extract 3% w/w
Traditional herbal remedy for symptomatic relief of mild psoriasis
Children: not recommended
Price: 30 g £3.85

Topical preparations for acne

Benzoyl peroxide

Brevoxyl P
Cream containing benzoyl peroxide 4% w/w
Treatment of mild to moderate acne
Price: 40 g £5.82

Oxy 5 or 10 P
Lotion containing benzoyl peroxide 5% or 10% w/w
Treatment of spots and acne
Price: 5% 30 ml £4.29, 10% 30 ml £4.59

Oxy On-The-Spot GSL
Cream containing benzoyl peroxide 2.5% w/w
Treatment of spots and pimples on the face
Children: not recommended for those under 6 years
Price: 20 g £3.99

Panoxyl 5 or 10 Acnegel P
Alcoholic gel containing benzoyl peroxide 5% or 10% w/w
Treatment of acne vulgaris
Price: 5% 40 g £2.66, 10% 40 g £2.98

Panoxyl Aquagel 2.5, 5 or 10 P
Aqueous gel containing benzoyl peroxide 2.5%, 5% or 10% w/w

continued overleaf

Panoxyl Aquagel 2.5, 5 or 10 P (*cont.*)
Treatment of acne vulgaris
Price: 2.5% 40 g £3.10, 5% 40 g £3.38, 10% 40 g £3.65

Panoxyl Wash 10 P
Lotion containing benzoyl peroxide 10% w/w
Treatment of acne vulgaris
Price: 150 ml £7.05

Panoxyl 5 or 10 Lotion P
Emulsion containing benzoyl peroxide 5% or 10% w/w
Treatment of acne vulgaris
Price: 5% 30 ml £2.56, 10% 30 ml £2.56

Panoxyl 5 Cream P
Cream containing benzoyl peroxide 5% w/w
Treatment of acne vulgaris
Price: 40 g £2.66

Benzoyl peroxide with antimicrobials

Quinoderm Cream P
Cream containing benzoyl peroxide 10% w/w, potassium hydroxy-quinoline sulphate 0.5% w/w
Treatment of acne
Price: 25 g £2.29, 50 g £4.39, Quinoderm cream 5 (benzoyl peroxide 5%) is also available: 50 g £3.90

Quinoderm Lotio-Gel 5% P
Emulsion/gel containing benzoyl peroxide 5% w/w, potassium hydroxyquinoline sulphate 0.5% w/w
Treatment of acne
Price: 30 ml £2.59

Nicotinamide

Papulex P
Hydro-alcoholic gel containing nicotinamide 4% w/w
Topical treatment of mild to moderate inflammatory acne vulgaris
Price: 60 g £14.06

Salicylic acid

Acnisal P
Solution containing salicylic acid 2%
Treatment of acne
Price: 177 ml £7.28

Sulphur

Clearasil Treatment Cream Regular (colourless) GSL
Cream containing sulphur 8% w/w, triclosan 0.1% w/w
Treatment and prevention of spots and acne
Price: 20 g £3.19 Also available as Cover Up

Preparations for warts and calluses

Salicylic acid

Bazuka Extra Strength Gel P
Water-resistant, film-forming gel containing salicylic acid 26% w/w
Treatment of verrucas, warts, corns and calluses
Price: 5 g £5.75

Bazuka Gel P
Water-resistant, film-forming gel containing salicylic acid 12% w/w, lactic acid 4% w/w
Treatment of verrucas, warts, corns and calluses
Price: 5 g £4.95

Carnation Callus + Caps GSL
Adhesive dressing with felt ring containing paste of salicylic acid 40% w/w
Removal of calluses
Not to be used by diabetics, pregnant women, people with severe circulatory disorders or those under 16 years of age except on medical advice
Price: 2 £1.50

Carnation Corn Caps GSL
Adhesive dressing with felt ring containing paste of salicylic acid 40% w/w
Removal of hard corns
Not to be used by diabetics, people with severe circulatory disorders or those under 15 years of age except on medical advice
Price: 5 £1.55, 10 £2.79

Carnation Verruca Treatment GSL
Adhesive felt pad with central well filled with paste containing salicylic acid 10% w/w
Treatment of verrucas
Not to be used by diabetics, people with severe circulatory disorders or children under 6 years of age except on medical advice
Price: 4 £4.15

continued opposite

Compound W P
Liquid containing salicylic acid 17% w/w

Treatment of common warts and verrucas

Children: not to be used in those under 6 years

Price: 6.5 ml £3.25

Duofilm P
Solution containing salicylic acid 16.7%, lactic acid 16.7%

Treatment of warts

Children: not recommended for those under 2 years

Price: 15 ml £3.43

Salactol Wart Paint P
Paint containing lactic acid 16.7% w/w, salicylic acid 16.7% w/w

Treatment of warts, verrucas, corns and calluses

Price: 10 ml £3.02

Salactac Wart Gel P
Gel containing lactic acid 4% w/w, salicylic acid 12% w/w

Treatment of warts, verrucas, corns and calluses

Price: 8 g £5.26

Scholl Callus Removal Pads GSL
Medicated plaster containing salicylic acid 40% w/w

Treatment of calluses

Children: not to be used for those under 16 years except on medical advice

Price: £1.59 per pack Corn removal pads are also available

Scholl Corn and Callus Removal Liquid P
Liquid containing camphor 2.8% w/v, salicylic acid 11.25% w/v

Children: not recommended for those under 16 years except on medical advice

Price: 10 ml £2.25

Scholl Removal Plasters GSL
Medicated plaster containing salicylic acid 40% w/w

continued overleaf

Scholl Removal Plasters GSL *(cont.)*
Treatment of corns

Children: not recommended for those under 16 years except on medical advice

Price: £1.59 per pack A washproof version is also available

Scholl Polymer Gel Corn Removers GSL
Medicated plaster containing salicylic acid 40% w/w

Treatment of corns

Children: not to be used for those under 16 years except on medical advice

Price: £3.99 per pack

Scholl Seal and Heal Verruca Removal Gel GSL
Liquid containing salicylic acid 11.25% w/v, camphor 2.8% w/v

Self-medication of common and plantar warts

Children: should not be used

Price: 5 ml £4.55

Scholl Verruca Removal System GSL
Medicated plaster containing salicylic acid 40% w/w

Treatment of common warts on the hands and feet

Children: not to be used on babies

Price: £4.15 per pack

Formaldehyde

Veracur GSL
Gel containing formaldehyde solution 0.75%

Treatment for warts, especially plantar warts

Price: 15 g £4.25

Glutaraldehyde

Glutarol P

Solution containing glutaraldehyde 10%

Treatment for warts

Price: 10 ml £3.65

Silver nitrate

AVOCA P

Caustic pencil containing silver nitrate 95%

Treatment for warts and verrucas

Price: £2.93

Shampoos and some other scalp preparations

Medicated shampoos

Alphosyl 2 in 1 Shampoo GSL
Medicated shampoo containing coal tar, alcoholic extract 5% w/w

Treatment of scalp disorders such as psoriasis, seborrhoeic dermatitis, scaling and itching (often associated with eczema) and dandruff

Price: 125 ml £2.99, 250 ml £5.69

Betadine Shampoo GSL
Shampoo containing povidone–iodine 4% w/v

Treatment of seborrhoeic conditions of the scalp associated with excessive dandruff, infected sores and impetigo

Children: not recommneded for those under 2 years

Price: 250 ml £4.10

Capasal Shampoo P
Shampoo containing salicylic acid 0.5% w/w, coconut oil 1% w/w, distilled coal tar 1% w/w

Treatment of dry, scaly scalp conditions such as seborrhoeic eczema, seborrhoeic dermatitis, dandruff, psoriasis and cradle cap in children

Price: 250 ml £8.27

Ceanel Concentrate P
Liquid containing undecenoic acid 1% w/w, cetrimide 10% w/w, phenylethyl alcohol 7.5% v/v

An adjunct in the management of psoriasis of the scalp, seborrhoeic dermatitis, dandruff and psoriasis of the trunk and limbs

Price: 50 ml £2.29, 150 ml £5.99, 500 ml £17.27

Denorex Anti-Dandruff Shampoo PO
Shampoo containing menthol 1.5% w/w, coal tar solution 7.5% w/w

Treatment of dandruff, psoriasis of the scalp and seborrhoeic dermatitis

Price: 125 ml £4.99 Denorex Anti-Dandruff Shampoo Plus Conditioner is also available 125 ml £5.09

continued opposite

Dentinox Cradle Cap Treatment Shampoo GSL
Shampoo containing sodium lauryl ether sulphosuccinate 6% w/w, sodium lauryl ether sulphate 2.7% w/w

Treatment of infant cradle cap and general care of infant scalp and hair

Price: 125 ml £2.25

Gelcotar Liquid GSL
Liquid containing strong coal tar solution 1.25% v/v, cade oil 0.5% v/v

Treatment of psoriasis, seborrhoeic dermatitis and dandruff

Price: 150 ml £2.94, 350 ml £5.85

Nizoral Dandruff Shampoo P
Shampoo containing ketoconazole 2% w/w

Prevention and treatment of scalp conditions, dandruff and seborrhoeic dermatitis

Price: 60 ml £5.75, 100 ml £8.75

Polytar AF P
Shampoo containing tar blend 1% w/w, zinc pyrithione 1% w/w

Treatment of scaling scalp disorders, including seborrhoeic dermatitis, psoriasis and dandruff. Also of value for the removal of ointments and pastes used in the treatment of psoriasis

Price: 150 ml £7.76

Polytar Liquid GSL
Shampoo containing tar blend 1% w/w

Treatment of scalp disorders such as psoriasis, dandruff, seborrhoeic eczema and pruritis. Also of value for the removal of ointments and pastes in the treatment of psoriasis

Price: 150 ml £2.72, 250 ml £3.93

Polytar Plus GSL
Liquid containing tar blend 1% w/w; also contains the hair conditioner polypeptide

Treatment of scalp disorders such as psoriasis, seborrhoea, pruritis and dandruff. Also of value for the removal of ointments and pastes used in the treatment of psoriasis

Price: 500 ml £7.76

Male-pattern baldness

Minoxidil

Regaine Extra Strength P
Solution containing minoxidil 5% w/v

Treatment of alopecia androgenetica in men

Not indicated for use in men under 18 or over 65 years of age

Price: 60 ml £29.95, 3 × 60 ml £59.95

Regaine Regular Strength P
Solution containing minoxidil 2% w/v

Treatment of alopecia androgenetica in men and women. Causes slowing of hair loss in patients with diagnosed male-pattern baldness

Not indicated for use in those under 18 or over 65 years of age

Price: 60 ml £24.95

Anti-infective skin preparations

Antifungal preparations

Benzoyl peroxide

Quinoped Cream P
Cream containing benzoyl peroxide 5% w/w, potassium hydroxy-quinoline sulphate 0.5% w/w

Treatment of athlete's foot

Price: 25 g £2.17

Clotrimazole

Candiden Cream P

Cream containing clotrimazole 1% w/w

Treatment of fungal infections such as vaginal thrush, candidal balanitis, candidal nappy rash, athlete's foot and ringworm

Price: 20 g £3.65

Canesten AF Cream GSL

Cream containing clotrimazole 1%

Treatment of athlete's foot

Price: 15g £3.20 Powder is also available: 30 g £3.49 Spray is also available: 25 ml £3.99

Canesten Cream P

Cream containing clotrimazole 1% w/w

Treatment of fungal and candidal skin infections, including candidal nappy rash, vulvitis and balanitis

Price: 20 g £4.15, 50 g £9.35

Canesten Powder P

Powder containing clotrimazole 1% w/w

Topical antifungal for fungal infections such as ringworm, intertrigo, nappy rash and body fungal infections

Price: 30 g £2.68 Spray is also available: 40 ml £8.79

Econazole nitrate

Ecostatin P

Cream containing econazole nitrate 1%

Treatment of fungal skin infections

Price: 15 g £2.63, 30 g £4.85

Pevaryl P

Cream containing econazole nitrate 1%

Treatment of fungal skin infections

Price: 30 g £4.67 Lotion is also available: 30 ml £5.87

Miconazole nitrate

Daktarin Cream P
Cream containing miconazole nitrate 2% w/w

Treatment of fungal and associated bacterial infections of the skin, including nappy rash

Price: 15 g £3.20 Powder is also available: 20 g £3.20

Daktarin Dual Action Cream GSL
Cream containing miconazole nitrate 2% w/w

Treatment of athlete's foot

Price: 15 g £3.20, 30 g £4.99 Powder is also available: 20 g £3.20

Daktarin Dual Action Spray Powder GSL
Spray powder containing miconazole nitrate 0.16% w/w

Treatment of athlete's foot

Children: should not be used
Price: 100 g £3.99

Tolnaftate

Mycil Athlete's Foot Spray GSL
Powder aerosol spray containing tolnaftate 1% w/w

Treatment of athlete's foot, dhobie itch (tinea cruris), prickly heat, and skin irritation caused by tenderness and sweating

Price: 150 ml £3.55

Mycil Ointment GSL
Ointment containing tolnaftate 1% w/w, benzalkonium chloride solution 0.1% w/w

Treatment of athlete's foot, dhobie itch, prickly heat, and skin irritation caused by tenderness and sweating

Price: 25 g £2.15

Mycil Powder GSL
Powder containing tolnaftate 1% w/w, chlorhexidine hydrochloride 0.25% w/w

Treatment of athlete's foot, dhobie itch, prickly heat, and skin irritation caused by tenderness and sweating

Price: 55 g £3.05

Scholl Athlete's Foot Cream GSL
Cream containing tolnaftate 1% w/w

Prevention and treatment of athlete's foot

Price: 25 g £1.99 Powder also available 75 g £2.95

Scholl Athlete's Foot Spray Liquid GSL
Aerosol spray containing tolnaftate 0.68% w/w

Prevention and treatment of athlete's foot

Price: 150 ml £3.39

Tinaderm Cream GSL
Cream containing tolnaftate 1% w/w

Treatment of athlete's foot

Price: 15 g £2.09 Tinaderm Plus Powder is also available: 50 g £3.35

continued overleaf

Tinaderm Plus Powder Aerosol GSL
Aerosol powder spray containing tolnaftate 0.9% w/w

Treatment of athlete's foot

Price: 75 g £3.45

Undecenoates

Mycota Cream GSL
Cream containing zinc undecenoate 20% w/w, undecenoic acid 5% w/w

Treatment and prevention of athlete's foot

Price: 25 g £1.99

Mycota Powder GSL
Powder containing zinc undecenoate 20% w/w, undecenoic acid 2% w/w

Treatment and prevention of athlete's foot

Price: 70 g £2.95

Mycota Spray GSL
Liquid aerosol spray containing undecenoic acid 3.9% w/w, dichlorophen 0.4% w/w

Treatment and prevention of athlete's foot

Price: 100 ml £3.19

Undecenoates with salicylic acid

Monphytol P
Paint containing chlorobutanol 3% w/v, methyl salicylate 25% w/v, salicylic acid 3% w/v, propyl salicylate 5% w/v, methyl undecenoate 5% w/v, propyl undecenoate 0.7% w/v

Treatment of athlete's foot

Price: 18 ml £2.83

Antiviral preparations

Acyclovir

Soothelip P

Cream containing acyclovir 5% w/w

Treatment of cold sore infection

Dosage given for adults and elderly only

Price: 2 g £4.49

Virasorb P

Cream containing acyclovir 5% w/w

Treatment of recurrent herpes labialis

Price: 2 g £4.15

Zovirax Cold Sore Cream P

Cream containing acyclovir 5% w/w

Treatment of herpes simplex virus infections of the lips and face

Price: 2 g tube £5.49, 2 g pump £5.99

Other cold sore preparations

Blisteze GSL

Cream containing ammonia solution strong 0.1% w/w, ammonia solution aromatic 6.04% w/w, liquefied phenol 0.494% w/w

Relief of cold sores, cracked lips or chapped lips

Price: 5 g £2.25

Brush Off Cold Sore Lotion GSL

Antiseptic paint containing povidone–iodine 10% w/v

Treatment of cold sores

Price: 8 ml £3.25

Lypsyl Cold Sore Gel P

Gel containing lidocaine hydrochloride 2% w/w, zinc sulphate 1% w/w, cetrimide 0.5% w/w

Symptomatic relief of cold sores

Children: not recommended except on medical advice

Price: 3 g £2.75

Parasiticidal preparations

Benzyl benzoate

Benzyl Benzoate Application BP (non-proprietary) GSL
Emulsion containing benzyl benzoate 25%

Treatment of scabies

Children: not recommended

Price varies

Malathion

Derbac M Liquid P
Liquid emulsion containing malathion 0.5%

Eradication of head lice, pubic lice and their eggs. Treatment of scabies

Children: not recommended for those under 6 months except under medical supervision

Price: 50 ml £3.79, 200 ml £9.25

Prioderm Cream Shampoo P
Shampoo containing malathion 1% w/w

Treatment of head and pubic lice infestations

Children: not to be used for those under 6 months except under medical supervision

Price: 40 g £4.55

Prioderm Lotion P
Alcohol-based lotion containing malathion 0.5% w/v

Eradication of head lice and pubic lice infestations and scabies

Children: not to be used in babies under 6 months except under medical supervision

Price: 50 ml £3.79, 200 ml £9.25

Quellada-M Cream Shampoo P
Shampoo containing malathion 1% w/w

Treatment of head lice and pubic lice infestations

Children: directions given for those aged 6 months and over

Price: 40 g £4.06

Quellada-M Liquid P
Liquid emulsion containing malathion 0.5%

Eradication of head lice, pubic lice and their eggs. Treatment of scabies

Children: directions given for those aged 6 months and over

Price: 50 ml £3.59, 200 ml £8.99

Suleo M Lotion P
Alcohol-based lotion containing malathion 0.5% w/v

continued overleaf

Suleo M Lotion P *(cont.)*
Eradication of head lice

Children: not recommended for those under 6 months except under medical supervision

Price: 50 ml £3.79, 200 ml £9.25

Permethrin

Lyclear Creme Rinse P
Cream rinse containing permethrin 1% w/w

Treatment of head lice infestations

Children: not recommended for those under 6 months except under medical supervision

Price: 59 ml £3.79, 2 × 59 ml £6.99

Phenothrin

Full Marks Liquid P
Aqueous liquid emulsion containing phenothrin 0.5% w/w

Treatment of head lice infestations

Children: not recommended for those under 6 months except under medical supervision

Price: 50 ml £3.79, 200 ml £9.25 A mousse is also available: 50 g £3.99, 150 g £9.25

Full Marks Lotion P
Alcoholic lotion containing phenothrin 0.2% w/v

Treatment of head lice and pubic lice infestations

Children: not recommended for those under 6 months except under medical supervision

Price: 50 ml £3.79, 200 ml £9.25

Topical circulatory preparations

Heparinoid-containing preparations

Hirudoid Cream P

Cream containing heparinoid 0.3% w/w

Treatment of superficial thrombophlebitis and the soothing relief of superficial bruising and haematoma

Children: not recommended for those under 5 years

Price: 50 g £2.39 A gel is also available

Lasonil P

Ointment containing per 100 g heparinoid 0.8% w/w

Treatment of bruises, sprains and soft-tissue injuries

Price: 40 g £1.90

Herbal preparations

Potter's Comfrey Ointment GSL

Ointment containing comfrey root liquid extract (2:1) 10% w/w

A traditional herbal remedy used for the symptomatic relief of bruises and sprains

Price: 55 g £4.05

Disinfectants and cleansers

Phenolics

Ster-Zac Powder P

Dusting powder containing hexachlorophene 0.33% w/w

Prevention of neonatal staphylococcal cross-infection and treatment of recurrent furunculosis

Price: 30 g £1.45

Antiperspirants

Aluminium salts

Anhydrol Forte P

Evaporative solution containing aluminium chloride hexahydrate 20% w/v

Local treatment of hyperhydrosis of armpits, hands or feet

Price: 60 ml £4.42

Driclor Solution P

Solution containing aluminium chloride hexahydrate 20% w/w

Treatment of excessive perspiration

Price: 60 ml £4.97

4 Is there a more cost-effective drug?

Making prescribing changes

Considerable savings have been made in many practices over the last few years by making prescribing changes. Fundholding was a stimulus to change, and recently the introduction of PCGs and PCTs has continued to encourage prescribing savings. The great majority of GPs agree that savings can be made. Only 15% of GPs surveyed in the Trent region reported that there was nothing they could do to contain prescribing costs without harming patients.[1] There was more uncertainty about changing patients' established medication when the reason was to keep costs down, with around 50% of GPs stating that they would find this difficult to do. Certain interventions are easier to conduct than others. The Northern Regional Health Authority encouraged various prescribing changes, and found that generic substitution was more easily implemented than other cost-saving measures.[2]

The work involved in making changes can be a drawback. One GP practice that made major changes on becoming fundholders found that of 100 intended changes, there were 70 successes and 16 additional consultations.[3] However, they were rewarded with an absolute saving of 24%.

Fear of jeopardising the GP–patient relationship is another reason why GPs may be unwilling to make changes. This does not seem to be a problem in practice provided that changes are made in a sensitive way. A qualitative survey of patients following a period when prescribing changes had been made reported that patients were willing to try cheaper treatments, and that dissatisfaction was primarily with the communication that patients received, rather than with the change itself.[3,4] Around 20% of patients reported being very unhappy with the changes, but none of the patients left the practice, and the study period covered a time when the list size in fact increased. Patients were found to accept changes provided that they were made in such a way as to make the individual patient feel valued.

Prescribing changes will never be 100% successful. The formulations do vary between different products and can account for some dissatisfaction. A few patients will always wish to stay on the original medication, however inconvenient and apparently unreasonable this appears to be. If the original medication is a parallel import product that is no longer available the situation can be particularly difficult! Practices will often be aware of patients for whom a change would be unacceptable, and these patients can be excluded from the process of change at the outset.

What types of changes should be chosen?

When deciding which prescribing changes to make, a number of factors need to be considered. A change which involves minimal effort, improves (or at least does not harm) patient care and provides significant savings is ideal – hence the relatively easy savings that are achieved as a result of increasing generic prescribing. Once these have been achieved, the specific changes introduced by practices will depend on their individual prescribing patterns, and Prescribing Analysis and Cost (PACT) data are ideal for identifying suitable targets (*see* Chapter 6).

Changes which result in improved patient care can easily be justified, and the use of cost-effective antibiotics, the use of simple analgesics instead of non-steroidal anti-inflammatory drugs (NSAIDs) and the use of low-dose proton-pump inhibitors (PPIs) can be included here. Changes from one drug to another can be justified, since the release of funds can be used to improve patient care in other areas. An example of this would be to switch to the most cost-effective PPI in order to fund the required increase in the use of lipid-lowering drugs. However, care must be taken to ensure that the drug being substituted is equally efficacious and does not have an increased frequency of adverse effects. New drugs are particularly problematic, as adverse effects of drugs are not fully understood until they have been widely used, and this is unlikely to be the case at launch.

Decisions on appropriate drug classes to be used can be difficult and frequently become ethical issues. Where the evidence points to the use of a cheap first-line drug, such as bendrofluazide in hypertension, it is relatively straightforward to recommend this. However, if the evidence points to a statistically marginally significant benefit for a more expensive drug class, does this mean that all patients should be treated with the more expensive drug, or is it acceptable to use the cheaper drug first to see if the response is sufficient? An example here would be the use of long-acting beta-adrenoceptors before high-dose steroids in asthma. Such decisions will be based on the evidence. What is the exact benefit? What is the additional cost? What other priorities for funding are there? Practices, PCGs and PCTs may well reach different decisions on such issues.

Basic information needed – drug charges to the practice

Before making any decisions on prescribing changes, an awareness of how drugs are priced by the Prescription Pricing Authority (PPA) and charged to the practice is necessary. The essential resource for this is the Drug Tariff. This tariff is updated monthly, and a copy should be available in each practice. Part VIII lists the basic prices for a range of drugs. This is not a complete list, and in cases where drugs are not included, the PPA costs the drug from the published price charged by the manufacturer, wholesaler or supplier. Proprietary drug prices are published in the *Monthly Index of Medical Specialties* (*MIMS*), which is again updated monthly. The *British National Formulary* (BNF) lists drug prices, but as this publication is only updated 6-monthly, the Drug Tariff and *MIMS* are better resources in this instance. Appliances are charged at the rate stated in Part IX of the Drug Tariff, and this is a complete list (appliances that do not appear in Part VIII are not allowed on FP10).

The drugs listed in Part VIII of the tariff are arranged in categories, and an explanation of these is given at the beginning of the section. This information is mainly for the use of pharmacists, but it is helpful for GPs to see which category a drug belongs to when generic prescribing (*see* below). Category A drugs are the widely used generics, and the tariff price is based on an average price for several manufacturers. Category B drugs are less widely used generics that are only available from a few suppliers. The tariff price of category C drugs is based on one particular manufacturer, and these are generally drugs for which generic products are not available. Category D drugs are those for which there are problems in supply, and the pharmacist will be paid for the particular brand supplied if the prescription is endorsed, otherwise the tariff price is applied. This category is likely to be abandoned.[5] Category E drugs are extemporaneously supplied products such as mixtures of creams or solutions which have been made up by the pharmacist.

Items that are not listed in Part VIII of the drug tariff are priced according to the pharmacist's endorsement, and there is no requirement for the pharmacist to supply the cheapest product available. For example, modified-release diclofenac tablets are not included in Part VIII of the April 2000 Drug Tariff, so for a generically written prescription the pharmacist will be paid for the product supplied, whether it is Voltarol, Volsaid or another product.

The pharmacist will generally dispense a generic product against a generic prescription when one is available and the drug is included in Part VIII of the drug tariff. To do otherwise would of course lead to financial loss, as the pharmacist will be paid the tariff price regardless of what they dispense (apart from category D items). An exception to this occurs when large companies are able to negotiate the purchase of proprietary products at reduced costs. In these instances proprietary products are dispensed against generic prescriptions. A common example is the dispensing of Ventolin against a generic prescription for salbutamol. This is not a problem for the primary care prescribing budget, as the practice will continue to be charged the Drug Tariff prices.

Types of prescribing changes

The following section describes the types of prescribing changes that can be made, and gives some examples of the scale of potential savings. Easy changes are presented first, and the majority of practices will have achieved savings in at least some of these areas. Practices which have already covered these areas will need to look to the other chapters in this book for further areas of potential saving.

Generic prescribing

Generic medicines are produced once the patent on a drug expires. Product licences are needed for generic medicines as for proprietary products, and the Medicines Control Agency requires evidence of safety, efficacy and quality before a licence can be granted. There is therefore no reason why generic medicines should be in any way inferior to branded products.[6]

National savings have been made in the past as generic prescribing has increased. PACT data show that the rate of generic prescribing has increased from 35% in 1985 to 70% in 1999 – very close to the government target of 72%. Further potential savings are now limited, although there are still some practices struggling to reach 40–50% generic prescribing. The level of GP acceptance of generic prescribing is high. A study in the Trent region reported that almost 90% of GPs felt that generic prescribing should be increased wherever this would save money without detriment to patient care.[1]

Despite the huge increase in generic prices in 1999, significant price differentials can be seen in the April 2000 Drug Tariff and *MIMS*, as shown in Table 4.1. It is likely that at least some of the price increases will be reversed,[5] leading to a reduction in the drugs bill and a restoration of larger differences between the cost of branded and proprietary products.

Table 4.1. Examples of savings achieved from generic prescribing

Branded product	Number of tablets/ units	Price (£) MIMS April 2000	Generic product	Price (£) April 2000 Drug Tariff Price	Difference per pack (£)	% price difference
Zyloric 100 mg	100	10.96	allopurinol 100 mg	2.34	8.62	79
Capoten 12.5 mg	56	10.56	captopril 12.5 mg	6.12	4.44	42
Frumil	28	5.91	co-amilofruse 5/40 mg	4.22	1.69	28
Ceporex 250 mg/5 ml 100 ml	1	3.19	cefalexin 250 mg/5 ml	2.58	0.61	19
Prozac	30	19.84	fluoxetine 20 mg	16.55	3.29	17
Zantac 150 mg	60	19.52	ranitidine 150 mg	17.67	1.85	9
Beconase nasal spray	1	4.01	beclometasone nasal spray	3.72	0.29	7
Zovirax 800 mg	35	75.11	acyclovir 800 mg	73.45	1.66	2

The disadvantages of using generic medicines are well known. The variation in appearance between products of different manufacturers and even between batches can lead to confusion among patients, and may potentially lead to non-compliance. However, in general, patients accept and understand the differences provided that practice staff and community pharmacists are supportive. The health authority will usually be able to advise on and possibly provide suitable patient information leaflets. It is well worth talking to local pharmacists prior to any widespread generic prescribing increases. Not only will they be able to prepare their stocks, but they will then be in a position to advise patients appropriately. Some GPs prescribe 'branded' generics (i.e. generic medicines produced by particular manufacturers). This does eliminate some of the variability in supply, but the practice cannot be recommended because the pharmacist is frequently unable to provide a particular brand of generic. Certain modified-release branded generics may be worth considering. If a drug is not included in Part VIII of the Drug Tariff, the use of branded generics (e.g. Volsaid Retard) can lead to savings. However, a close eye must be kept on drug prices, and much greater savings can usually be made by not prescribing modified-release preparations (see below).

Generic prescribing is recommended not only for its cost-saving aspect but also for reasons of quality. It is very easy to forget the components of products which are prescribed by their proprietary name. The generic name usually indicates the pharmacology of the drug, and teachers in undergraduate and postgraduate education refer to products by their generic name. Products should be prescribed generically from the time of their launch. This also ensures that once the patent expires, any savings are made immediately and the patient does not have to get used to a new name. However, certain products should not be prescribed generically. Drugs which have a narrow therapeutic index can cause problems, as the different brands have varying characteristics which can lead to slight differences in absorption. Thus generic prescribing of lithium is not recommended. Generic prescribing of anti-epileptics is controversial, although in practice it does not seem to cause problems.[7] Cyclosporin should not be prescribed generically – there are considerable differences in bioavailability between Neoral and Sandimmun. Modified-release preparations are best prescribed by proprietary name, especially diltiazem and nifedipine. Some drug combinations are best prescribed by proprietary name. For example, certain cream combinations can be very confusing when prescribed generically. On the whole, however, the majority of products can be prescribed generically.

Generic prescribing will of course only lead to savings if generic products are available. Using the Drug Tariff will very quickly indicate whether savings are possible – category C drugs are based on proprietary brands. Another very useful resource is the list of potential price savings produced by the PPA, which is included in the 'prescribing toolkit' and is available on the NHS net to PCGs/PCTs and health authorities.

Multiple low doses

It is becoming increasingly common to reduce the price differences between different strengths, so that to prescribe two low-dose tablets is more expensive than prescribing one high-dose tablet. Some preparations, such as Zantac, double in price as the dose doubles. Examples where this is not the case are listed in Table 4.2. It can be seen that the price per milligram varies according to the dose of the preparation. The situation can arise where a patient increases the dose initially by taking two tablets, and this is continued. Changing this type of prescription is unlikely to result in large savings, but it is a point to bear in mind when undertaking medication reviews.

Table 4.2. Unit price of drugs at different doses

Drug	Pack size	Dose	Price (£) (April 2000)	Price (£)/ 100 mg
Zocor	28	10 mg	18.03	6.4
	28	20 mg	29.69	5.3
	28	40 mg	29.69	2.7
	28	80 mg	29.69	1.3
Istin	28	5 mg	11.85	8.5
	28	10 mg	17.7	6.3
Losec	28	10 mg	18.91	6.8
	28	20 mg	28.56	5.1
Viagra	4	25 mg	16.59	16.6
	4	50 mg	19.34	9.7
	4	100 mg	23.5	5.9

Dose

Very significant savings can be made by ensuring that an appropriate dose is prescribed, and practices have made substantial savings just by reducing the dose of PPIs. A dose reduction is often accompanied by a change to a more cost-effective drug in the same class (*see* below). Many practices spend more on omeprazole 20 mg than on any other drug, so a shift of a large proportion of those patients to a lower dose will have a significant effect. In practice, many patients can be controlled on the lower dose and the change should be accompanied by lifestyle advice. In order to ensure that medicines are not wasted on future patients, many patients who are new to PPIs can be initiated on the lower dose. Intermittent therapy with PPIs is another possibility. It has been shown to be effective in the management of about 50% of patients with uncomplicated gastro-oesophageal reflux disease.[8]

The National Institute for Clinical Excellence has issued guidance on heartburn and indigestion. NHS savings of around £50m are predicted from a more circumspect use of proton-pump inhibitors and this includes the use of maintenance doses following symptom control in gastro-oesophageal reflux disorder.[9]

Savings can also be made, albeit on a smaller scale, by ensuring that patients take the lowest dose of drugs such as sumatriptan which will control their symptoms. Many patients were initiated on the 100 mg dose before the 50 mg dose became available, and they may never have tried the lower dose.

Atenolol and co-tenidone are worth considering in this respect. The majority of hypertensive patients will be managed on 50 mg, but the *BNF* reports that higher doses are no longer considered necessary. It could be that patients who have been taking atenolol for some years have not tried the lower dose.

Asthma is another area in which doses can sometimes be reduced. The British Thoracic Society guidelines[10] recommend a stepwise reduction in treatment once control is established.

The percentage savings for these changes, using the April 2000 Drug Tariff, are listed in Table 4.3.

Doses prescribed for the elderly also need to be considered. Cohen[11] has reviewed the data on the use of lower doses in the elderly, and his findings with regard to effective low doses for a range of commonly used drugs are listed in Table 4.4. He advocates starting the elderly on low doses

Table 4.3. Savings that can be achieved by using lower-dose drugs

Drug	High dose	Pack size	Cost of high dose (£)	Low dose	Cost of low dose (£)	Saving (£)	% saving
Omeprazole	20 mg	28	28.56	10 mg	18.91	9.65	34
Lansoprazole	30 mg	28	28.15	15 mg	14.21	13.94	50
Sumatriptan	100 mg	6	48	50 mg	29.7	18.3	38
Atenolol	100 mg	28	2.12	50 mg	1.69	0.43	20
Beclometasone* MDI	800 µg	1	19.61	400 µg	8.71	10.9	56

*The beclometasone savings are based on a change from 200 µg to 100 µg monitored-dosage inhaler (MDI).

Table 4.4. Effective reduced initial drug doses for older patients[11]

Drug	Standard initial dose	Lower-dose alternative
Atorvastatin calcium (Lipitor)	10 mg/day	5 mg/day
Captopril (Capoten)	50–75 mg/day	12.5 mg once daily or bid
Celecoxib (Celebrex)	10 mg bid	5 mg bid
Conjugated oestrogens (Premarin)	1.25 mg/day	0.3–0.625 mg/day
Diclofenac sodium (Voltaren)	100–200 mg/day	75 mg/day
Enalapril (Vasotec)	5 mg/day	2.5 mg/day
Fexofenadine HCl (Allegra)	60 mg bid	20 mg tid or 40 mg bid
Fluoxetine HCl (Prozac)	20 mg/day	2.5, 5 and 10 mg/day
Hydrochlorthiazide	25 mg/day	12.5 mg/day
Ibuprofen (Motrin et al.)	400–800 mg tid to qid	200 mg tid to qid
Lovastatin (Mevacor)	20 mg/day	10 mg/day
Metoprolol tartrate (Lopressor)	100 mg/day	50 mg/day
Misoprostol (Cytotec)	200 µg qid	50–100 µg qid
Nefazodone HCl (Serzone)	100 mg bid	50 mg bid
Nizatidine (Axid)	150 mg bid or 300 mg at bedtime	25–100 mg bid or 100–200 mg at bedtime
Omeprazole (Prilosec)	20 mg/day	10 mg/day
Ondansetron HCl (Zofran)	8 mg bid to tid	1–4 mg tid
Ranitidine HCl (Zantac)	150 mg bid	100 mg bid
Simvastatin (Zocor)	20 mg/day	5 or 10 mg/day
Trazodone HCl (Desyrel)	150 mg/day	25–100 mg/day

initially in order to avoid adverse drug effects. Consideration can also be given to reducing doses. This is another ideal prescribing change – one which results in improved patient care as well as cost savings.

These types of drug changes need to be managed in different ways according to the drug. With some drugs it is possible to make changes over almost all of the practice population, while with others a more gradual approach is appropriate, and changes can be made at medication review (*see* Chapter 5).

Choice of formulation

Formulations such as transdermal patches, modified-release formulation, topical preparations and combination preparations tend to be more expensive than standard tablets. They are usually prescribed for reasons of compliance, and in some instances this is valid. However, standard tablets can frequently be used first line. In some cases standard tablets can have positive therapeutic advantages. For example, tolerance can be a problem with nitrate patches, skin irritation can occur with hormone replacement therapy patches, and the patient who forgets a once daily dose can be more at risk than someone who forgets to take one tablet of a twice daily regime. Compliance is a particular concern with regard to patients who are taking more than three or four medications daily, or if the frequency is more than twice daily. Compliance with pain-relieving medication is unlikely to be such a problem as compliance with antihypertensives, and in the case of diclofenac 50 mg three times daily, the omission of the midday dose will be of clinical benefit if the symptoms remain controlled. If it is necessary for symptoms to be controlled over an extended period, it is often possible to choose an inherently longer-acting drug rather than a modified-release formulation. If diclofenac 50 mg leads to pain through the night, then naproxen could be used. The *BNF* classifies diclofenac and naproxen as being of intermediate risk with regard to serious upper gastrointestinal side-effects.

Modified-release isosorbide mononitrate has been targeted by practices, and there are reports of the transfer of patients' medication to ordinary-release isosorbide mononitrate being successful, with no increase in symptoms or adverse effects in the majority of patients.[12,13]

The price of combination products needs to be monitored closely. In the past, preparations such as Tylex were considerably cheaper to prescribe as paracetamol and codeine separately, and this price differential may well be restored. Combination products do of course have inherent disadvantages other than cost, as the dose of the two drugs cannot be easily adjusted. For example, if side-effects developed with Tylex, as commonly occurs, the dose of codeine could not be reduced without also reducing the dose of paracetamol.

These types of prescribing change and the potential savings are listed in Table 4.5.

Cost-effective drug choices within a class

Where several drugs are available within a drug class the potential exists to make savings by changing to the cheapest drug and there is evidence that fundholders have employed this method to make savings.[14] Work on formularies tends to concentrate on this aspect. Unfortunately, decisions as to which drugs to choose can be difficult due to lack of evidence. Head-to-head trials on the particular drugs of interest are not always available. A decision also needs to be made as to whether the drug decided upon is for new patients, or whether patients' long-term medication will be changed. Using the drug of choice for new patients is very straightforward and controls costs, but it does not result in actual savings. Changing long-term medication will result in savings, but needs to be done much more carefully than the simpler changes (e.g. to generic prescribing).

Before any decision is made, the evidence (including any recently published trials as well as reviews) needs to be considered. Claims made for newer products need to be appraised critically in order to determine whether there is direct evidence for any stated advantages being of clinical relevance. For instance, is the difference in half-life between amlodipine and felodipine clinically relevant? Side-effects may also be an issue. Clarithromycin results in fewer gastrointestinal side-effects, but to what extent and is this worth the additional cost? Studies have examined the cost-effectiveness of the newer NSAIDs,[15] but reached no firm conclusions and the *Drug and Therapeutics Bulletin* recommends the use of ibuprofen as the first-line NSAID.[16] GPs may be concerned that cheaper options will not be well received by patients. One study found that ibuprofen was as highly regarded as other NSAIDs when used in similar circumstances.[17]

Considerable savings have been realised by changing patients' medication from 20 mg omeprazole to 15 mg lansoprazole. One report projected savings of close to £8000 per annum in one practice,[18] while another projected savings of £6300 per annum.[19]

Some examples of these types of changes, together with potential savings (April 2000 Drug Tariff and *MIMS*), are shown in Table 4.6.

Table 4.5.   Examples of savings achieved through a change in formulation type (April 2000 Drug Tariff and MIMS prices)

Original product	Cost for 28 days (£)	Lower-cost product	Cost for 28 days (£)	Monthly saving (£)	% saving
Voltarol SR 75 mg bd	17.35	Diclofenac 50 mg tds	9.18	8.17	47
Volsaid retard 75 mg bd	12.38	Diclofenac 50 mg tds	9.18	3.2	26
Voltarol SR 75 mg bd	17.35	Naproxen 500 mg bd	8.57	8.78	51
Monomax 40 mg od	8.31	Isosorbide mononitrate 20 mg bd	3.22	5.09	61
Imdur 60 mg od	11.14	Isosorbide mononitrate 20 mg bd	3.22	7.92	71
Imdur 60 mg od	11.14	Isosorbide mononitrate 40 mg bd	6.46	4.68	42
Nuvelle TS	10.51	Elleste duet	3.24	7.27	69

Table 4.6. Savings achieved through the choice of cost-effective drugs within a class

Original drug	Quantity	Cost (£)	Lower-cost drug option	Cost (£)	Saving (£)	% saving
Ranitidine 150 mg bd	56	16.49	Cimetidine 400 mg bd	15.04	1.45	8.8
Omeprazole 20 mg od	28	28.56	Lansoprazole 30 mg od	28.15	0.41	1.4
Omeprazole 20 mg od	28	28.56	Lansoprazole 15 mg od	14.21	14.35	50.2
Omeprazole 20 mg od	28	28.56	Pantoprazole 20 mg od	14.21	14.35	50.2
Amlodipine 5 mg od	28	11.85	Felodipine 5 mg od	8.12	3.73	31.5
Losartan 50 mg od	28	17.23	Candesartan 8 mg od	14.95	2.28	13.2
Fluticasone 2 × 50 µg bd	200 dose	9.74	Beclometasone 2 × 100 µg bd	8.71	1.03	10.6
Sertraline 50 mg od	28	16.2	Fluoxetine 20 mg od	15.45	0.75	4.6
Sumatriptan 50 mg	6	29.7	Zolmitriptan 2.5 mg	24	5.7	19.2
Clarithromycin 250 mg bd	14/28	11.24	Erythromycin 2 × 250 mg bd	3.08	8.16	72.6
Diclofenac 50 mg tds	84	9.18	Ibuprofen 600 mg tds	5.26	3.92	42.7
Nabumetone 2 × 500 mg od	56/84	18.11	Ibuprofen 600 mg tds	5.26	12.85	71

Drugs of limited clinical value

In 1994[20] the Audit Commission identified a range of drugs which show limited evidence of effectiveness, including topical NSAIDs, cough suppressants and expectorants, and peripheral vasodilators. The *BNF* now identifies certain products as 'less suitable for prescribing', and these include analgesics with low doses of opioids. The arguments over some of these drugs have continued for some years. In the case of topical NSAIDs, it appears that they have a greater effect than that of placebo. However, if an analgesic is required, paracetamol together with a topical rubefacient is likely to be as effective. If an anti-inflammatory effect is needed, then regular doses of an oral NSAID over several days are likely to be more effective. However, this is a pragmatic approach, and firm evidence along these lines is lacking. Nevertheless, *MeReC* concludes that the high level of prescribing is not justified by the available evidence.[21]

Cough suppressants and expectorants are infrequently prescribed these days, although some practices find that it is useful to prescribe them as an alternative to antibiotics. Customers who find these preparations or topical NSAIDs helpful can of course purchase them.

Analgesics such as co-codamol (8/500 mg), co-dydramol and co-proxamol are very widely prescribed, despite the fact that the *BNF* states that the advantages of these products over paracetamol alone have not been substantiated. They can cause problems with opioid side-effects, especially in the elderly, and can complicate the treatment of overdose.

Examples of these potential savings are listed in Table 4.7 (April 2000 Drug Tariff and *MIMS*).

Table 4.7. Potential savings by not using drugs of limited clinical value

Original product	Cost (£)	Lower cost option	Cost (£)	Saving (£)	% saving
100 Co-codamol 8/500 mg	1.76	100 paracetamol	0.59	1.17	66
100 Co-dydramol 10/500 mg	1.99	100 paracetamol	0.59	1.4	70
100 Co-proxamol	1.59	100 paracetamol	0.59	1.0	63
Ibuprofen gel 5% 30 g	2.42	transvasin 40 g	0.89	1.53	63
Ibuprofen gel 5% 30 g	2.42	100 paracetamol	0.59	1.83	76
Ibuprofen gel 5% 30 g	2.42	transvasin + paracetamol	1.48	0.94	39

Cost-effective drug class

Savings made by changing the class of drug used are probably the most difficult type to achieve, yet the price differences between drug classes can be enormous. For example, the difference between bendrofluazide and losartan is over 12-fold. Hypertension is a particularly good example, as national guidelines support the use of thiazides and beta-blockers first line. There have also been reports questioning the safety of calcium-channel blockers,[22] yet their use has increased year on year.[23] The situation might have been different if drug representatives had been selling bendrofluazide!

The use of NSAIDs is another important area. Guidelines recommend the use of simple analgesics first line for osteoarthritis, and there is evidence that NSAIDs can sometimes be withdrawn. In one general practice, 24 of 38 patients who attempted to withdraw NSAIDs and substitute alternative analgesics achieved this after 4 months.[24]

A third relevant area is treatment of depression. This is rather more controversial, there being a considerable difference of opinion as to whether tricyclic antidepressants or SSRIs should be chosen first line. There is widespread agreement that tricyclics are as efficacious as SSRIs, and a suggestion that they may be more so in severe depression. However, tricyclics are more difficult to prescribe, as the dose needs to be adjusted upwards. At least one recent review concludes that tricyclics still have an important place in the treatment of depression.[25] Various cost-effectiveness analyses have been attempted but have given different conclusions based on the assumptions made in the analysis.[26]

Table 4.8 lists some examples of the types of costs involved. Price differences can be considerable, and tend to be higher than for other changes. For example, a change from Voltarol SR 75 mg to Volsaid Retard gives a saving of £4.97 per month, to diclofenac 50 mg gives a saving of £8.17 per month and to paracetamol 500 mg gives a saving of £16.03. Some of the changes would involve cost containment rather than actual savings. For instance, it would not be appropriate to change long-term medication for antidepressants.

Table 4.8. Examples of savings made by changing the class of drug used

Original drug	Cost for 28 days (£)	Lower-cost option	Cost for 28 days (£)	Saving (£)	% saving
Amlodipine 5 mg od	11.85	Bendrofluazide 2.5 mg od	1.36	10.49	89
Adalat LA 20 mg od	8.15	Bendrofluazide 2.5 mg od	1.36	6.79	83
Voltarol SR 75 mg bd	17.35	Paracetamol 500 mg × 2 qds	1.32	16.03	92
Ibuprofen 400 mg tds	4.73	Paracetamol 500 mg × 2 qds	1.32	3.41	72
Sertraline 50 mg od	16.2	Imipramine 25 mg × 4 bd	3.3	12.9	80
Fluoxetine 20 mg od	15.45	Imipramine 25 mg × 4 bd	3.3	12.15	79

References

1 Avery AJ et al. (2000) Do GPs working in practice with high or low prescribing costs have different views on prescribing cost issues? Br J Gen Pract. **50**: 100–4.

2 Roberts SJ et al. (1997) Prescribing behaviour in general practice: the impact of promoting therapeutically equivalent cheaper medicines. Br J Gen Pract. **47**: 13–18.

3 Dowell JS et al. (1995) Changing to generic formulary: how one fund-holding practice reduced prescribing costs. BMJ. **310**: 505–8.

4 Dowell JS et al. (1996) Rapid prescribing change: how do patients respond? Soc Sci Med. **43**: 1543–9.

5 Pharmaceutical Journal (2000) Government to scrap category D and impose generic price cuts. Pharm J. **264**: 642.

6 Drug and Therapeutics Bulletin (1997) Generic medicines – can quality be assured? Drug Ther Bull. **35**: 9–11.

7 MeReC Bulletin (1996) Effective generic prescribing. MeReC Bull. **10**.

8 Bardham KD et al. (1999) Symptomatic gastro-oesophageal reflux disease: double-blind controlled study of intermittent treatment with omeprazole or ranitidine. BMJ. **318**: 502–7.

9 Ferriman A (2000) NICE issues guidance for heartburn and indigestion. BMJ. **321**: 197.

10 British Thoracic Society (1997) The British guidelines on asthma management: 1995 review and position statement. *Thorax.* **52** (**Supplement 1**): S1–21.

11 Cohen JS (2000) Avoiding adverse reactions. Effective lower-dose drug therapies for older patients. *Geriatrics.* **55**: 54–6, 59–60, 63–4.

12 Weatherhead S and Holden K (1999) Pharmacist-managed therapeutic substitution of modified-release oral nitrates. *Pharm J.* **263**: R21.

13 Macgregor S (2000) Angina management – are patients adequately controlled? *Primary Care Pharm.* **1**: 55–7.

14 Baines DL *et al.* (1997) General practitioner fundholding and prescribing expenditure control. Evidence from a rural English health authority. *Pharmacoeconomics.* **11**: 350–8.

15 McCabe CJ *et al.* (1998) Choice of NSAID and management strategy in rheumatoid arthritis and osteoarthritis. The impact on costs and outcomes in the UK. *Pharmacoeconomics.* **14**: 191–9.

16 Drug and Therapeutics Bulletin (1998) Meloxicam – a safer NSAID? *Drug Ther Bull.* **36**: 62–4.

17 Hawkey CJ *et al.* (2000) Ibuprofen versus other non-steroidal anti-inflammatory drugs: use in general practice and patient perception. *Aliment Pharmacol Ther.* **14**: 187–91.

18 Russell R and Anderson C (1999) An assessment of the impact of a model for a community pharmacist-supported practice-based audit of gastrointestinal repeat prescribing. *Pharm J.* **263**: R60.

19 Johnstone P (1999) Assessing the success of a therapeutic substitution of a proton pump inhibitor. *Pharm J.* **263**: R20–21.

20 Audit Commission (1994) *A Prescription for Improvement. Towards More Rational Prescribing in General Practice.* HMSO, London.

21 MeReC Bulletin (1997) Topical non-steroidal anti-inflammatory drugs: an update. *MeReC Bull.* **8**.

22 MeReC Bulletin (1998) Safety of calcium-channel blockers. *MeReC Bull.* **4**.

23 Siegel D and Lopez J (1997) Trends in antihypertensive drug use in the United States: do the JNC V recommendations affect prescribing? Fifth Joint National Commission on the detection, evaluation and treatment of high blood pressure. *JAMA.* **278**: 1745–8.

24 Swift GL and Rhodes J (1992) Are non-steroidal anti-inflammatory drugs always necessary? A general practice survey. *Br J Clin Pract.* **46**: 92–4.

25 Judd F and Boyce P (1999) Tricyclic antidepressants in the treatment of depression. Do they still have a place? *Aust Fam Physician.* **28**: 809–13.

26 Henry JA and Rivas CA (1997) Constraints on antidepressant prescribing and principles of cost-effective antidepressant use. Part 2. Cost-effectiveness analysis. *Pharmacoeconomics.* **11**: 515–37.

5 Could the prescribing system be more efficient?

This chapter examines how prescribing takes place and is guided in a practice. Three general areas are covered, namely practice organisation, tools to guide prescribing decisions, and interaction with patients.

Practice organisation

Prescribing lead

Someone in the practice – and not necessarily a GP – needs to take the lead with regard to prescribing. This individual needs to monitor PACT data as it arrives so that changes to practice can be made as necessary, and they need to be aware of educational opportunities or other available support so that the practice can make full use of any resources which are available. They can act to co-ordinate any pharmaceutical or other support that the practice receives. Responsibility for different aspects of prescribing can be allocated to different members of staff. The practice manager is often in an excellent position to encourage generic prescribing, a pharmacist could be responsible for formulary development or update, and receptionists could be given responsibility for ensuring that all repeat prescriptions requested are actually needed. A policy should be developed for dealing with drug representatives. Will one person see all reps and communicate any relevant information, or will reps be invited to practice meetings, after which any information that they have provided is critically appraised? It is important that prescribing is organised and not left to chance.

Repeat prescribing

The organisation of repeat prescribing is of vital importance. Repeat prescriptions have been estimated to account for 75% of all prescribing and 81% of prescribing costs.[1] There is a vast potential for drug wastage from inappropriate repeats, inappropriate quantities prescribed (both the overall quantity and the co-ordination of quantities of different drugs), and repeats being requested when they are not actually needed.

A prescription request for many items with all of the available items ticked needs to be regarded with a degree of suspicion. Some elderly patients, due to confusion or poor eyesight, find it simplest to order everything rather than select those items that are actually needed. An audit by community pharmacists in Bromley (unpublished data) found that a small proportion of requested medicines were not required. With increased awareness, pharmacists and receptionists can help to reduce this wastage.

The prescription length of repeat medications can be a source of irritation to both pharmacists and GPs. Pharmacists are reimbursed for each pre-scription dispensed, so that a practice changing from a 28-day to a 56-day repeat-prescribing cycle may significantly affect the pharmacist's income. A GP often sees the production of numerous 28-day prescriptions as waste-ful and time-consuming. With regard to costs to the primary care prescribing budget, in theory the length of the repeat-prescribing cycle makes no differ-ence to overall costs. In practice it is likely to have an influence, as any medicines returned to the pharmacy cannot be reused. Therefore if a patient changes their medication just after having a prescription dispensed, then the medication is wasted and without exception community pharmacists are aware that this happens. A judgement therefore needs to be made as to what is appropriate for particular patients. In general, 28 days is seen as ideal, 56 days is acceptable, and 6 months is common for items such as the con-traceptive pill. Prescriptions such as one in which a 12-month supply of simvastatin was ordered are inappropriate, despite pressure from a patient who had to pay prescription charges.

The quantities of different drugs on a prescription may not be co-ordinated, and the term 'inequivalence' has been used to describe this situation. A patient faced with a 28-day supply of one drug and a 30-day supply of another is likely to order both drugs every 28 days. The cost of the two tablets can be very significant over time and for several patients. Of course it would be helpful if the manufacturers could decide exactly how long a month is! However the majority of drugs are packed in multiples of 28, and only a few are still marketed in packets of 30. The pharmacist is able to split calendar packs (see clause 10 C in the Drug Tariff), although this can be made problematic by the requirement to provide patient information leaflets. Nevertheless, the majority of prescriptions could be co-ordinated, and the help of pharmacists and receptionists can be enlisted. This is one aspect of prescribing which can be considered at medication review.

Several points need to be covered in order to ensure that inappropriate medicines are not prescribed on repeat. A report published in 1996 pro-vided evidence that the control of repeat prescribing was inadequate in many practices.[2] First, a tight system of authorising repeats is needed. Repeats should only be authorised by the prescriber, and the practice should agree on which drugs are unsuitable for repeat prescribing. Decisions as to whether and when PPIs, anxiolytics/hypnotics, hay fever medications, antibiotics and sip feeds should be put on repeat should be made. Secondly, a compliance check should be in place. This is usually a facility on computerised prescribing systems, but is easily ignored. Thirdly, a foolproof system for medication review should be in place. An achievable period for review needs to be agreed upon, and normally the prescribing computer system is able to monitor this and indicate when a review is needed. Receptionists must be aware of the importance of review, and they should not be in a position to override the computer system.

A medication review requires the presence of the patient in order to cover aspects such as compliance, side-effects, and OTC medication use. It is also an appropriate time to consider whether drugs can be discontinued (*see* Chapter 2) or whether more cost-effective drugs can be substituted (*see* Chapter 4), and to consider whether the existing therapy adheres to current guidelines. The following set of indicators of long-term prescribing appropriateness has been developed by the National Primary Care Research and Development Centre,[3] and these should be considered at a medication review.

1 The indication for the drug is recorded and upheld in the *British National Formulary (BNF)*.

2 The reason for prescribing a drug of 'limited value' is recorded and valid.

3 Compared to alternative treatments in the same therapeutic class, which are just as safe and effective, the drug prescribed is either one of the cheapest or a valid reason is given for using alternatives.

4 A generic drug is prescribed if one is available.

5 If a potentially hazardous drug–drug interaction combination is prescribed, the prescriber demonstrates knowledge of this hazard.

6 If the total daily dose is outside the range stated in the *BNF*, the prescriber gives a valid reason for this.

7 If the dosing frequency is outside the range stated in the *BNF*, the prescriber gives a valid reason for this.

8 If the duration of therapy is outside the range stated in the *BNF*, the prescriber gives a valid reason for this.

9 Prescribing for hypertension adheres to the evidence-based guidelines in the *BNF*.

It can therefore be seen that medication review is a fairly time-consuming process and unrealistically short review times should not be set. It is unlikely that medication review can be undertaken opportunistically when a patient presents (e.g. with an infection), as time needs to be set aside for the process. Medication review in elderly patients taking multiple medications is particularly valuable, and studies have shown significantly reduced rates of prescribing following review.[4,5]

Tools to guide prescribing decisions

Formularies

What do doctors think?

As long ago as 1990 the Department of Health recommended the development of practice formularies.[6] The implementation of this has been variable. Some GP practices are not convinced of their worth, some claim lack of resources as an obstacle, while others have developed a formulary which has been left to gather dust. However, many have been enthusiastic and have implemented and regularly update their formulary. A survey examining the attitudes of GPs showed that over 75% of GPs agreed that using a prescribing formulary can help to control costs without detriment to patients. However, this figure decreased to around 50% when GPs were asked whether the benefits of developing a practice formulary outweighed the time and effort involved.[7]

Do formularies result in prescribing changes?

There is evidence that formularies do result in prescribing changes, and a few reports will be mentioned here. One practice reports a saving of 24% following the introduction of a generic formulary, although this practice was just becoming a fundholder, and the change in generic prescribing alone was substantial (37% to 58%).[8] In another report, 10 general practices in Lincolnshire developed a formulary for NSAIDs. The mean number of different drugs used decreased, and the percentage of daily defined doses of the three commonly used drugs increased compared to control practices in which a formulary had not been developed.[9] A district drug formulary was developed by 50 general practices in Bedfordshire,[10] and prescribing was compared to all other general practices in the county. The proportion of formulary drugs increased in cardiovascular, musculoskeletal and obstetrics/gynaecological areas, and the number of items prescribed per prescribing unit decreased in musculoskeletal, nervous and nutrition/haematological areas, leading to savings of £3000 per doctor per year. The magnitude of any savings made as a result of introducing a formulary will of course depend on the prescribing characteristics of the particular practice. A practice with very cost-effective prescribing and operating without a formal formulary cannot expect to make large savings, and its costs may even increase. However, the benefits of producing a formulary extend far wider than cost-saving. GPs find the educational process of producing a formulary very valuable, and it can lead to the production of patient management guidelines with an improvement in the overall quality of patient care.

What type of formulary?

Formularies can be produced at different levels, and there are advantages and disadvantages to each. Practice formularies should involve all prescribers in their development, and prescribers are therefore likely both to be committed to the formulary and to make prescribing changes. However, this does mean that regular practice meetings must be arranged to develop and update the formulary. A PCG/PCT formulary involves less time commitment from each practice, and has the potential to increase cost-effective prescribing over many practices. The downside is less educational involvement and less commitment to make changes. The district-wide formulary in Bedfordshire[10] resulted in considerable prescribing changes, but in this case each practice had chosen to take part. It is possible that a PCG/PCT formulary would be less effective. The third level of formulary is a joint primary/secondary care formulary, and several areas have started this process, including Bromley. This has similar disadvantages to the PCG/PCT formulary with regard to commitment and education, but has the major advantage of influencing secondary care prescribing. Hospital-led prescribing has a considerable influence on GP prescribing. One practice found that hospital-led prescribing accounted for at least 38% of the total cardiovascular drug spend.[11] Therefore the involvement of both primary and secondary care in producing a formulary has the potential to improve overall cost-effectiveness. Perhaps the ideal would be a joint primary/secondary formulary that could be adapted by individual practices to their own practice formulary.

The style of formulary can vary considerably. Some practices find a simple list of drugs adequate, while others prefer to identify first- and second-line drugs. Indications are useful, but care should be taken not to make the formulary too elaborate. There is no advantage in having a 'mini-BNF' which is never updated. Some formularies become a series of patient management guidelines. The style will depend on the preferences of the prescribers, and all styles are valid and can be effective.

Similarly, the choice of an electronic or paper formulary will depend upon individual circumstances. Computerised prescribing systems include a formulary option which can be individualised and easily updated. WeBNF could be considered, especially for a joint primary/secondary care formulary, and again it can be easily updated. (The Royal Pharmaceutical Society can be contacted for information on *WeBNF*.)

Process of formulary development

Formularies are usually developed as a result of a series of meetings of prescribers to agree upon individual drug choices. The meetings should ideally be attended by all prescribers who intend to use the formulary. This is obviously not possible for a district-type formulary, and in this case a method of consultation on decisions needs to be developed to enable all prescribers to be involved. In addition to prescribers, it is useful for community pharmacists and prescribing advisers to attend. Nurses are now included in the category of prescribers, but it is valuable to have specialist non-prescribing nurses attending particular sessions. Local experts give a valuable input if this can be arranged, and in particular a microbiologist is useful for the sessions on anti-infectives. Obviously for a joint primary/secondary care formulary, hospital specialists and pharmacists need to attend particular meetings.

The meetings need a lead person – frequently a pharmacist – to ensure that the meetings are well organised, and to keep the momentum going. It is useful to circulate drug information prior to a meeting. This can refer to the *BNF* and include product summary sheets and recent reviews, or key papers. The frequency of meetings needs to be agreed. Monthly meetings are common, but less frequent meetings may be more appropriate for some practices. It is better to achieve a high rate of attendance at meetings that are widely spaced than to rush through a formulary with little input from some prescribers.

The meetings may focus on therapeutic areas in the *BNF*, or they may be disease orientated. It is worth starting in an area where benefits are likely to be seen fairly quickly to provide encouragement to the group. There is therefore no need to progress through the *BNF* in order, although gastro-intestinal drugs are often a good starting point.

The scope of the formulary should be agreed. Concentrating on several *BNF* chapters is usually adequate, as there is no need to cover all areas in a primary care formulary. An 80% rate of adherence to a formulary is usually aimed for and is achievable.[12] There will always be occasions when the formulary drug is not appropriate for a particular patient.

Agreement as to how drugs will be chosen should be discussed. Drug choice should be based on efficacy, safety and cost, and the drug formulation must be considered. The Bedfordshire district formulary[10] included drugs for which the majority of group members favoured inclusion, although decisions reached by consensus are more usual in practice formularies.

New drugs and updating of the formulary

Formulary development should not be seen as a 'one-off' process. Meetings need to continue on a regular basis, albeit less frequently, to update the formulary as new drugs are launched or new evidence becomes available on existing drugs. The lead person, with input from other members, needs to decide which aspects will be reviewed.

It is likely that new drugs with significant clinical or cost implications will be considered by area prescribing committees composed of members of the health authority, PCGs/PCTs and the acute and community trusts. Increasingly, the National Institute for Clinical Excellence (NICE) will also review new drugs. As decisions are made by these groups they will need to be incorporated into the practice formulary. However, other new drugs of less significance, such as a new drug in an existing class, will need to be considered by the practice and decisions made as to whether to include them.

Monitoring the formulary

The meetings to update the formulary can also be used to monitor adherence. Without continuous reinforcement of a formulary it can easily be forgotten. A group practice in Ireland found that the high level of formulary prescribing that was prevalent during formulary production was not maintained following its launch, probably due to lack of reinforcement.[13]

Adherence to the formulary can be measured using PACT data, and this would normally be done at the level of the PCG/PCT or health authority. This can give a complete picture of which drugs are being used, but there may be a delay before this data becomes available. Alternatively, practice prescribing systems can be used. It may not be necessary to monitor all formulary drugs, as it is often possible to identify particular drugs for which non-adherence is likely (i.e. drugs which had been fairly frequently used before the introduction of the formulary, and that were not selected for inclusion). Depending on the drug, 80% adherence to the formulary will take a variable length of time to achieve. For some conditions it will not be appropriate to change the existing medication. However, a decrease in non-formulary drugs and an increase in formulary drugs should be seen over time.

Guidelines

Function of guidelines

The National Primary Care Research and Development Centre/National Prescribing Centre has defined the function of guidelines as being 'to facilitate practitioners in the delivery of appropriate care, based on the best available evidence, not to mandate or outlaw particular treatments'. Guidelines also play an important part in the rationing process.[14] Guidelines such as those for IVF treatment and for lipid-lowering drugs are evidence based, but the result is to restrict treatment to those who are likely to benefit most – some individuals will be excluded by the guidelines who may benefit from treatment even though the level of benefit is likely to be limited. Norheim[15] states that clinical practice guidelines can be mechanisms for rationing and tools for improving the quality of rationing decisions, but cautions against economic or political decisions being disguised as clinical decisions.

Which guideline?

Numerous clinical guidelines are available, and there will be few occasions when completely new local guidelines need to be developed. The National Primary Care Research and Development Centre/National Prescribing Centre suggest that existing guidelines should be assessed by considering the following:[3]

1 Assessing appropriateness.

- Is the guideline appropriately defined and not too broad or non-specific?

- Can the guideline help to change clinical behaviour?

- Will the guideline achieve the desired outcome(s) when used in patient management?

- Does the guideline take into account the feasibility of the interventions?

- Does the guideline address any barriers to its implementation that may exist (e.g. professional resistance to change)?

- Does the guideline reflect the views of patients and the community in the recommended interventions where relevant?

- Does the guideline take account of the resource implications of the proposals?

2 Assessing robustness.

- Is the guideline practical and usable?

- Does the guideline explicitly identify the important major decisions relevant to patients?

- Was the guideline developed in a systemic way and is it truly representative?

- Does the guideline explicitly state or contain references for the evidence upon which the recommendations are based?

- Does the guideline include an explicit process to seek expert opinion during the development of the guidelines?

- Has a development process which includes representation for the potential users of the guideline (e.g. GPs) been instituted?

Norheim[15] also discusses the quality of guidelines, and suggests that the following factors should be considered when assessing the acceptability of guidelines.

- Are the inclusion and exclusion criteria transparent, and is their rationale stated explicitly?

- Is this information accessible to all key stakeholders in a written and understandable form?

- Are the exclusion and inclusion criteria discussed with reference to medical criteria, costs and opportunity costs, and non-medical criteria such as age, productivity, social status and gender?

- Are the reasons for exclusion and inclusion stated in a form that can be recognised as valid and relevant?

Developing local guidelines

Local guidelines are often developed when no nationally approved guidelines are available. This can be done at the practice level (e.g. the use of sip feeds in particular nursing homes) or more usually it will be done at the PCG/PCT or health authority level, and GPs will be asked to participate in the production of these guidelines.

The process of guideline production is similar to that of formulary development in that a group needs to be formed and include a lead, appropriate specialists, users of the guideline and, if appropriate, members of the public (perhaps representing voluntary user groups). The evidence must be reviewed by a thorough search of the literature before the guideline itself is put together.

The findings of a study by Grol and colleagues[16] of the attributes of guidelines that influence their use should be borne in mind when putting a guideline together. Evidence-based recommendations with explicit descriptions of the scientific evidence were found to be better followed in practice than recommendations that were not based on scientific evidence. Those authors conclude that 'guidelines should be compatible with existing values among the target group and not be too controversial. They should not demand too much change to existing routines and should be defined precisely, with specific advice on actions and decisions in different cases. They should be compatible with current values and routines'.

It is normal for both potential users of the guidelines and experts in the particular therapeutic area to be consulted about any new guidelines. In the case of a practice guideline where all users may well have participated in guideline production, this part of the process will be much simpler.

Implementation and monitoring of guidelines

Guidelines that are produced outside the practice – whether they are national or local guidelines – should ideally be considered by the practice in order to discuss any changes to the practice that are needed and how these will be managed. This is a good opportunity for a multiprofessional educational meeting, and it can involve nurses, pharmacists and practice staff.

Prescribing systems can sometimes be used to help implementation. An automated computer query has been tested in a randomised control trial and was shown to increase the switch from calcium-channel blockers for hypertension to first-line agents.[17] Computer programs can be helpful. The risk of coronary heart disease can be assessed with a computer disc provided with the joint UK recommendations on prevention of coronary heart disease.[18] This program is also available in some GP computer-prescribing systems.

Monitoring the use of guidelines is important. PACT data can be used but have limitations in this respect, as they indicate usage of particular drugs but not who they have been given to or the indication. Audit is therefore a more valuable tool, and there are many standard audit packs available to practices which can be adapted for local use. Audit need not be complex, and it would reinforce the use of a guideline to monitor one aspect in a simple audit.

Cost savings

Guidelines can result in cost containment (e.g. the use of a newly introduced drug), cost increases (e.g. the introduction of a lipid-lowering guideline) or in cost savings (e.g. a guideline on osteoarthritis). An improvement in the quality of care can be expected from most guidelines, and even where overall costs increase, certain elements of a guideline may result in savings (e.g. a reduction in the use of lipid-lowering drugs in patients with low levels of risk for coronary heart disease, a reduction in the use of antidepressants in patients with mild depression, or a step-down in therapy for asthmatics).

Guidelines which could reasonably be expected to save money on implementation include the following:

- guidelines on the treatment of osteoarthritis advising on first-line treatment with simple analgesics

- hypertension guidelines recommending first-line use of thiazides and beta-blockers

- antibiotic guidelines on the treatment of minor ailments

- guidelines recommending the appropriate use of sip feeds and food fortification

- guidelines on the use of hypnotics and antipsychotics in nursing and residential homes

- guidelines on the use of PPIs.

PRODIGY (Prescribing RatiOnally with Decision support In General practice studY)

PRODIGY is a computerised decision-support system that can be used when prescribing for an individual patient.[3] It provides advice on prescribing and suggests options for non-drug treatment. Evidence-based guidelines are incorporated into the system and patient advice leaflets can be produced. If desired, the practice's own formulary can be incorporated. PRODIGY is available to all practices and has been shown to result in prescribing changes. The use of this system would considerably simplify the production of a practice formulary and could limit the requirement for local guidelines. However, once adopted it is still valuable for the practice to meet to consider the different elements of the system and to make any local amendments.

Interaction with patients

There is evidence that around 50% of people who suffer from chronic diseases do not take their medicines in fully therapeutic doses and so do not derive the optimum benefits from treatment.[19] This is a huge waste of resources that leads to extra costs of treating the avoidable consequent morbidity. Non-compliance is also likely to lead to direct drug wastage, with patients disposing of medicines which they have not taken.

In 1997, a report produced by the Royal Pharmaceutical Society[19] described concordance as a new liberal model of the relationship between patient and prescriber based on negotiation between equals. The aim of concordance is defined as 'to optimise health gain from the best use of medicines compatible with what the patient desires and is capable of achieving'. Non-concordance therefore becomes the failure of the patient and the prescriber to reach a therapeutic agreement.

The concept of concordance differs from compliance or adherence, where the emphasis is on the patient taking the medicines in the way that the prescriber has suggested. There has been considerable research on compliance, although this has not resulted in evidence of interventions which result in long-term improvements in compliance.[19]

Important factors that determine whether a patient will take their medication have been shown to depend on the physical and social vulnerability of the patient and on the failure of communication between prescriber and patient.[19] The communication failure is largely due to a disparity of beliefs between doctors and patients. The types of beliefs that patients have about their medicines have been identified by sociological research and a few of them are listed below:[19]

- concern about becoming immune over time (e.g. to antibiotics)

- anxiety about the unnaturalness of manufactured medicines and fear that taking them will harm the body or mind

- fears of addiction and dependence

- discrepancies between the doctor's and the patient's perceptions of risk.

Steel[20] showed that doctors would initiate antihypertensives at a lower level of risk than the general public when both groups were presented with the same risk information. Doctors cannot therefore assume that their patients will share their opinion as to whether or not treatment for hypertension is worthwhile.

A study by Britten and colleagues[21] in the West Midlands and South East England identified misunderstandings between patients and doctors. Various categories of misunderstanding were identified, such as patient information unknown to the doctor and conflicting information. All of the misunderstandings were associated with lack of patient participation in the consultation in terms of the voicing of expectations and preferences, or the voicing of responses to the doctor's decisions and actions. They all had the potential for adverse outcomes such as non-compliance. Britten and colleagues state that doctors seemed to be unaware of the relevance of patients' ideas about medicines for successful prescribing.

A further study[22] analysing GP–patient consultations showed that patient agendas were often not voiced. These included concerns about side-effects, not wanting a prescription, and worries about the possible diagnosis. Problem outcomes such as the non-use of prescriptions or non-adherence to treatment were seen as a result of this.

Horne and colleagues have developed a model which shows that high beliefs about the necessity of prescribed medicines lead to high compliance, and concern about the potential adverse effects leads to non-compliance.[23] An explanation of the importance of taking the medication should therefore be given to patients. For example, it may not be sufficient for patients to be told that they have high blood pressure or high cholesterol levels, without giving an explanation of the consequences of these conditions.

The recommendations in the report on compliance[19] included further research, improved professional education and an increase in public awareness. In the interim, whilst awaiting the results of further research, it is important for prescribers to be aware that patients' beliefs are likely to be very different to their own, and that they will make decisions as to whether or not to take their medication on the basis of their own beliefs. Attempts should therefore be made to explore these beliefs and to try to reach an agreement with the patient as to how a particular medicine will be taken.

References

1 Harris CM and Dajda R (1996) The scale of repeat prescribing. *Br J Gen Pract.* **46**: 649–53.
2 Zermansky AG (1996) Who controls repeats? *Br J Gen Pract.* **46**: 643–7.
3 Cantrill J *et al.* (1999) Improving quality in primary care. Supporting pharmacists working in primary care groups and trusts. National Primary Care Research and Development Centre and National Prescribing Centre. University of Manchester, Manchester.
4 Hamdy RC *et al.* (1995) Reducing polypharmacy in extended care. *South Med J.* **88**: 534–8.
5 Fillit HM *et al.* (1999) Polypharmacy management in Medicare-managed care: changes in prescribing by primary care physicians resulting from a program promoting medication reviews. *Am J Manag Care.* **5**: 587–94.
6 Department of Health (1990) *Improving Prescribing – The Implementation of the GP Indicative Prescribing Scheme. Section 13.* Department of Health, London.
7 Avery AJ *et al.* (2000) Do GPs working in practice with high or low prescribing costs have different views on prescribing cost issues? *Br J Gen Pract.* **50**: 100–4.
8 Dowell JS *et al.* (1995) Changing to generic formulary: how one fundholding practice reduced prescribing costs. *BMJ.* **310**: 505–8.
9 Avery AJ *et al.* (1997) Do prescribing formularies help GPs prescribe from a narrower range of drugs? A controlled trial of the introduction of prescribing formularies for NSAIDs. *Br J Gen Pract.* **47**: 810–14.

10 Hill-Smith I on behalf of the South Bedfordshire Practitioners' Group (1996) Sharing resources to create a district drug formulary: a countryside controlled trial. *Br J Gen Pract.* **46**: 271–5.

11 Edgar S and Girvin B (1999) The effect of hospital-led prescribing on the cardiovascular drug budget of a fundholding general practice. *Pharm J.* **264**: 292–4.

12 Kamps GB *et al.* (2000) Adherence to the guidelines of a regional formulary. *Fam Pract.* **17**: 254–60.

13 Wyatt TD *et al.* (1992) Short-lived effects of a formulary on anti-infective prescribing – the need for continuing peer review. *Fam Pract.* **9**: 461–5.

14 Grimshaw JM and Hutchinson A (1995) Clinical practice guidelines – do they enhance value for money in healthcare? *Br Med Bull.* **51**: 927–40.

15 Norheim OF (1999) Healthcare rationing – are additional criteria needed for assessing evidence-based clinical practice guidelines? *BMJ.* **319**: 1426–9.

16 Grol R *et al.* (1998) Attributes of clinical guidelines that influence use of guidelines in general practice: observational study. *BMJ.* **317**: 858–61.

17 Rossi RA and Every NR (1997) A computerised intervention to decrease the use of calcium-channel blockers in hypertension. *J Gen Intern Med.* **12**: 672–8.

18 British Cardiac Society, British Hyperlipidaemia Association, British Hypertension Society and British Diabetic Association (1998) Joint British recommendations on prevention of coronary heart disease in clinical practice. *Heart.* **80**(**Supplement 2**): S1–29.

19 Royal Pharmaceutical Society of Great Britain (1997) *From Compliance to Concordance. Achieving Shared Goals in Medicine-taking.* Royal Pharmaceutical Society of Great Britain, London.

20 Steel N (2000) Thresholds for taking antihypertensive drugs in different professional and lay groups: questionnaire survey. *BMJ.* **320**: 1446–7.

21 Britten N *et al.* (2000) Misunderstandings in prescribing decisions in general practice: qualitative study. *BMJ.* **320**: 484–8.

22 Barry C (2000) Patients' unvoiced agendas in general practice consultations: qualitative study. *BMJ.* **320**: 1246–50.

23 Horne R *et al.* (1999) The Beliefs about Medicines Questionnaire (BMQ): the development and evaluation of a new method for assessing cognitive representations of medication. *Psychol Health.* **14**: 1–24.

6 Obtaining help and sources of information

The task of ensuring that the most effective use is made of a primary care prescribing budget can be time-consuming and may involve literature searches, formulary development, guideline production, medication review clinics, making prescribing changes on computer systems, informing patients of changes, audit, analysing prescribing data, and so on. Chapter 5 discussed making full use of existing practice staff. This chapter will examine first who can help from outside the practice, secondly the sources of prescribing data, and thirdly some useful sources of drug information.

Getting help from outside the practice

Pharmacists

Almost without exception all practices will have access to pharmacists to help with prescribing. Various types of pharmacist will be available. Most PCGs/PCTs have prescribing advisers – a survey published in May 2000 found that 87% of PCGs had advisers.[1] In addition, health authority prescribing advisers have been in place for some years. The level of advice will vary considerably, with some advisers being able to spend significant amounts of time in a practice (especially the practices projecting an overspend!), and others perhaps only able to offer an annual visit. At the very minimum, advisers will be able to identify areas of prescribing which have the potential for making savings as well as areas where the quality of prescribing needs to be investigated.

If prescribing advisers have only limited time available for a practice it may be possible to employ either hospital or community pharmacists on a sessional basis. The type of support that can be provided is described in a document produced by the National Prescribing Centre and the Department of Health.[2] Pharmacists are involved in a range of activities, including formulary development,[3] medication review[4,5] and patient clinics.[6]

Some practices now have their own practice pharmacist, and their role in the practice can be wide-ranging, from developing repeat-prescribing protocols to domiciliary visits, and from monitoring drug therapy to discharge and outpatient prescription requests.[7]

In addition to pharmacists working with GPs in the practice, it is important to include the local community pharmacists in work on prescribing. They are in an excellent position to support any prescribing changes when talking to patients, provided of course that they are aware of the changes taking place and the rationale behind them. They often find it difficult to attend practice meetings but may be able to arrange this if some notice is given. Alternatively, GPs often call into pharmacies to explain changes which are taking place (a phone call made first to ask when the pharmacy is likely to be quiet can be useful).

PCGs are now recognising the potential of community pharmacists in prescribing. Hayes and Harlington plans to pay pharmacists to complete intervention forms as part of their normal working day in order to help practices to meet incentive targets.[8]

Pharmaceutical industry

The pharmaceutical industry offers considerable resources to individual practices, PCGs/PCTs and health authorities for training and prescribing support. Some health authorities have developed a range of joint projects in areas such as medication review of PPIs, use of ACE inhibitors in heart failure, and the development of depression guidelines. Practices have used company support to change prescribing to a more cost-effective product, to a different formulation of a particular drug, and to help to introduce CFC-free inhalers. Financial support for such projects is not tied to the use of a particular product, and often the prescribing changes are made by nurses working independently of the company.

Such projects can work well provided that both parties are aware of the other's objectives. The objective of a pharmaceutical industry is to increase sales of their product. They are often happy to sponsor projects which raise awareness of a particular therapeutic area (e.g. depression or lipid-lowering), as a general increase in prescribing is likely to include their product. They would not invest money in this way for no return. However, this is frequently not a problem for the GP or health authority. In the case of lipid-lowering, an increase in appropriate prescribing is the aim of both the prescriber and the industry.

An individual practice that is considering whether to work with the pharmaceutical industry in this way should contact their PCG/PCT, as there is likely to be guidance available on working with the industry, and it would be wise to ensure that the planned project does not conflict with other initiatives.

Sources of prescribing data

Prescribing data are essential to identify areas of potential change, to identify potential patients for prescribing changes, and as a starting point for formulary development. These data are also needed to monitor change following an intervention such as the introduction of a practice formulary or clinical guidelines, a medication review clinic, or a prescribing audit. There are three possible sources of data, namely the GP practice, the community pharmacist and the PPA, and each has its own specific advantages and disadvantages.

Practice prescribing data

Practice prescribing data are up to date and readily available. They are only useful if all prescribers use the computer for acute and repeat prescriptions. This may be a problem with nurse prescribers, depending on how they record their prescriptions, and the same is true for prescriptions written whilst visiting patients.

The information is on prescriptions that are produced for patients, rather than on prescriptions that are dispensed, and is therefore likely to be an overestimate of spend. It could be of interest to compare practice data with PPA data for, say, antibiotics in order to determine the size of the discrepancy.

A major strength of practice prescribing data, unlike data from the PPA or community pharmacies, is that the patient can be identified, the dose prescribed is accessible and so too is the indication. For instance, all patients using high-dose PPIs can be identified. The usefulness of having the indication alongside the prescribing data will vary between practices according to how the computer is used. It will be particularly useful in a practice which uses a restricted set of diagnostic read codes routinely. This type of information is invaluable in audit and can answer questions such as 'what proportion of asthmatics use inhaled corticosteroids?' or 'what doses of diclofenac are used for osteoarthritis in the elderly?'.

MIQUEST is a tool that is being developed to use practice computer systems to provide anonymised, clinically-based datasets.[9] This will be particularly valuable at the PCG/PCT or health authority level to inform work on needs assessment and the production of quality indicators.

Community pharmacy patient medication records

Community pharmacy prescribing data are less often used in this context. Their particular advantages are that up-to-date information is available and they provide data on what has been dispensed rather than on what has been prescribed. This can be useful when looking at compliance – it is not unknown for a GP to write regular prescriptions for inhaled corticosteroids and for the patient not to collect them.

A report on an antimicrobial prescribing audit describes how a community pharmacy is used to provide data.[3] The community pharmacist, who dispensed 70% of the practice's prescriptions, attended practice meetings in which an antibiotic formulary and guidelines were developed. Monthly reports on antibiotics dispensed were then produced from the community pharmacy patient medication records. The advantage of this over data from the PPA is that the information was produced without a time lag. A further advantage is the involvement of the community pharmacist, who played an important role in encouraging change.

A restriction on the use of community pharmacy data is that it is not normally complete for a particular practice.

PACT (Prescribing Analysis and CosT)

The PPA produce PACT data from the prescriptions which have been dispensed. The PPA receives the prescriptions from community pharmacies and costs them in order to reimburse pharmacists for the cost of the drugs. It follows that PACT is able to provide information on the drugs dispensed, the quantity and the number of prescriptions, but not on dosage, indication or patient details. For instance, it cannot provide the costs of prescriptions for the elderly or for children. It is nevertheless an extremely useful data source that gives highly accurate and complete data. The delay in obtaining the data is at least one month, and is frequently considerably longer.

GPs are very familiar with the PACT standard report, which is sent to all practices quarterly. This gives spend in the highest-costing *BNF* chapters, sections and drugs for the practice. There are comparisons with regional and national averages, so that a practice can see whether they are relatively high or low cost. In addition to cost information, data are given on the number of items. This can be useful for comparing changes over time, but the comparison with an average will have more to do with the practice's repeat-prescribing system than anything else (e.g. a practice with a 28-day cycle will have a relatively large number of items). Items can be particularly valuable as a measure of volume of antibiotic prescriptions where the majority of prescriptions are for acute conditions.

Quarterly nurse-prescribing reports are also available and include all items in the nurse-prescribing formulary. These are useful both for monitoring changes over time and for comparing prescribing between GPs and nurses.

Cost comparisons with the regional or national average are based on the use of prescribing units (*see* Chapter 1). Thus two practices which spend an identical amount of money on an identical number of patients will have different costs per prescribing unit depending on the practice character-istics, and one of them will be classed as a higher-cost prescriber than the other.

PACT catalogue reports can be ordered either for the whole practice or for individual prescribers. They consist of a list of drugs dispensed given in *BNF* order, and were used for prescribing analysis prior to the development of electronic versions of PACT. They are still useful for individual prescriber data.

Electronic versions of PACT (ePACT and ePACTnet) are available at the PCG/PCT and health authority. Trends over time and comparisons between practices can be easily obtained from these systems.

The limitations of using the number of items as a measure of prescribing volume have been largely overcome by the use of defined daily doses (DDDs) and average daily quantities (ADQs). Defined daily doses are developed and maintained by the World Health Organization. Each drug has a dose which represents an average maintenance daily dose for its main indication in adults – it may not be a real dose but it is a measurement of the volume of prescribing. ADQs are similar, but have been adjusted to suit prescribing behaviour in England. For instance, a comparison of the number of ADQs per prescribing unit of benzodiazepines between practices is a useful method of comparing benzodiazepine prescribing. In contrast, a comparison of items per prescribing unit will vary between practices because of vari-ations in the average quantity of drugs prescribed per item, as well as any real variation in the level of prescribing.

Sources of drug information

Regularly updated references

BNF

This is an essential reference source which is updated on a 6-monthly basis. It is a useful starting point for developing local formularies and guide-lines. The system of marking some drugs as 'less suitable for prescribing' is valuable when considering formulary choices. It gives a good indication of drug prices, but other sources of this information are updated more frequently.

Drug Tariff

This is updated monthly and includes drug prices for commonly used drugs (Part VIII). Community pharmacy and dispensing doctor reimbursement is based on these prices. Other information that is provided includes the fees paid to pharmacists, the limited list, the borderline substance list and appliances allowed on NHS prescription.

MIMS (Monthly Index of Medical Specialties)

This is updated monthly and is a useful source of drug prices not included in the Drug Tariff. Various tables may be of use in formulary development, such as the list of hormone replacement products. These tend to assume that branded products will be used, which in the case of hormone replacement therapy is not a problem, but the table on potential skin sensitisers does not include aqueous cream or emulsifying ointment.

Association of the British Pharmaceutical Industry (ABPI) compendium of data sheets and summaries of product characteristics

This is updated annually and provides valuable information, for instance, for formulary development. It is now available online at www.emc.vhn.net

OTC Directory

This is updated annually and produced by the Proprietary Association of Great Britain. It is a useful source of information on OTC medicines, and includes prices, indications and dosages. It is available free to GP practices and other relevant organisations.

Clinical Evidence

This is updated 6-monthly and provides evidence of the effectiveness of common clinical interventions based on literature searches. It is produced by the BMJ Publishing Group and the American College of Physicians and American Society of Internal Medicine.

Guidelines – summarising clinical guidelines for primary care

This is updated three times a year. It is a valuable reference source that summarises guidelines in different therapeutic areas. Guidelines recommended by the NHS Executive are identified. It is available free to GP practices and other relevant organisations.

Evidence-based reviews

MeReC/Drugs and Therapeutics Bulletin

Twelve issues of each bulletin are produced each year, which are an excellent source of information for formulary development and guidelines. They are available commercially on CD-ROM together with the *BNF*, as well as the usual paper format.

Bandolier/IMPACT

Bandolier is a newsletter supporting evidence-based practice, and it includes useful drug information together with information on healthy living. IMPACT gives examples of evidence-based practice. Both are available free on the Internet at http://www.jr2.ox.ac.uk/Bandolier/

Cochrane Collaboration

These are systematic reviews of randomised controlled trials and reviews of other evidence which are updated regularly. The reviews are available free on the Internet at http://hiru.mcmaster.ca/cochrane/default.htm An example is a review on non-aspirin, non-steroidal anti-inflammatory drugs for osteoarthritis of the knee.

NHS Centre for Reviews and Dissemination

These bulletins on effectiveness are available free on the Internet at http://www.york.ac.uk/inst/crd/ Recent drug-related issues include *'Systematic review of wound care management (2) Dressings and topical agents used in the healing of chronic wounds' (Health Technology Assessment Report)* and *'Drug treatment of essential hypertension in older people' (Effectiveness Matters)*.

NICE (National Institute for Clinical Excellence)

The website available at http://www.nice.org.uk contains the NICE appraisals.

Audit protocols

Clinical governance research and development unit

Audit protocols are available online at http://www.le.ac.uk/cgrdu and include protocols on angina, hypertension and asthma.

Royal Pharmaceutical Society of Great Britain

These audit protocols are aimed at community pharmacists but also include multiprofessional audits such as an audit on repeat prescribing. They are available online at http://www.rpsgb.org.uk/audhome.htm

Searching the literature

PubMed

Free access to MEDLINE is made available by the United States National Institutes of Health and found at www.ncbi.nlm.nih.gov/PubMed/ It is very easy to use.

Google

This is a useful, fast search engine available at http://www.google.com/

Turning Research into Practice (TRIP) database

This is available on the NHS net at http://www.gwent.nhs.gov.uk/trip/. Guidelines and sources of evidence on effectiveness can be searched.

Other sources of information

UK Drug Information Pharmacists Group (UKDIPG) website

This can be found at www.ukdipg.org.uk and it provides information about new drugs (some information is only available to registered users).

Druginfozone

The South Thames Drug Information Service website is available at http://www.druginfozone.org or on the NHS net at http://nww.gstt.sthames.nhs.uk/affiliated/dizone/index.htm It contains the following:

- One Stop Reference Shop – a list of independent evidence-based drug-related reviews listed in *BNF* therapeutic category order

- Primary Care Journal Watch, which summarises drug-related journal reports and is a useful resource for keeping up to date on prescribing issues

- new drug reviews, such as a review of the glitazones in diabetes mellitus.

Medical information departments at pharmaceutical companies

Pharmaceutical company medical information departments are useful sources of information on specific products.

National Prescribing Centre

The website at http://www.npc.co.uk (or http://nww.npc.ppa.nhs.uk on the NHS net) has information resources including 'A Short Guide to Prescribing Terms' and 'Improving Quality in Primary Care'.

Health authorities, PCGs and PCTs

Information on new drugs both before and after launch is sent to the health authority and PCGs/PCTs. Examples of reviews include 'New Drugs in Clinical Development', produced by the National Prescribing Centre.

References

1 Pharmaceutical Journal (2000) Pharmacists making progress in PCGs. *Pharm J.* **264**: 745.
2 National Prescribing Centre and NHS Executive (1998) *GP Prescribing Support, a Resouce Document and Guide for the New NHS.* National Prescribing Centre and NHS Executive, London.
3 Lau SF (1999) A community pharmacist's input in an antimicrobial prescribing audit. *Pharm J.* **263**: R26.
4 Mackie CA *et al.* (1999) Randomised controlled trial of medication review in patients receiving polypharmacy in general practice. *Pharm J.* **263**: R7.
5 Sodha M *et al.* (1999) Evaluation of the role and effectiveness of pharmacists working with general practitioners. *Pharm J.* **263**: R39.
6 Weatherhead S and Holden K (1999) Pharmacist-managed therapeutic substitution of modified-release oral nitrates. *Pharm J.* **263**: R21.
7 Bradley M (1999) The role of the full-time practice pharmacist. *Primary Care Pharmacy.* **1**: 14–15.
8 Pharmaceutical Journal (2000) PCG pays pharmacists for prescription interventions. *Pharm J.* **264**: 5.
9 Cantrill J *et al.* (1999) *Improving Quality in Primary Care. Supporting Pharmacists Working in Primary Care Groups and Trusts.* National Primary Care Research and Development Centre and National Prescribing Centre. University of Manchester, Manchester.

Index

Proprietary (trade) names are printed in *italic* type.